Stories Are Forever

Published in 2016 by Canterbury Christ Church University
North Holmes Road, Canterbury, Kent CT1 1QU

ISBN 978-1-909067-56-1

Creative Writing Workshops are part of the Community Arts and Education programme offered by the School of Childhood and Education Sciences at Canterbury Christ Church University (CCCU). These diverse groups are made up of students with varying degrees of writing experience.

For the spring 2016 anthology, we are pleased to offer you a collection of short stories and life writing.

April Doyle
Tutor and Editor

Contents

You Only Live Once by John O'Connor	p7
One Person in the Crowd by Carol Hyde	p17
On His Majesty's Secret Service by Susan Morley	p21
Here and Now by Valerie Moffit	p31
It's in the Tealeaves by Jo Gamgee	p41
Gettin' Over You by Caroline Cannons	p51
A Regular Portion of Broccoli by Mo Wright	p59
Bond to the Rescue by Mo Wright	p61
Home from the Jungle by Frederic Stansfield	p63
Beachy Head by Carole Lynch	p71
The Man with the Golden Heart by Carol Hyde	p79
Beige by Emma Collins	p83
I Should've Gone to Marks by Judy Walker	p89
Live and Let Die by C A Nitzsche	p93
Author biographies	p101

You Only Live Once

John O'Connor

When she'd agreed to go with him, her first thought had been shoes. Flats for most occasions - long periods sitting on the bus, then short flurries of trudging, followed by more sitting-stills. But then she'd need something for the evenings too. Though her heart was pleased that he'd actually asked her to accompany him on the three day coach tour of Bond movie locations, taking in southern England and the near-continent, her head was full of misgivings. For a start she hated the whole Bond thing; misogynist nonsense would be a fair summation of her feelings. But things had become so strained between them and she appreciated that this was his way of trying to bring them closer together. But - a coach tour? What happened to a romantic weekend for two in Paris? It all seemed rather puerile and one-dimensional, and morally questionable too; having raised two independently-minded daughters and been successful in her own career, the whole Bond-girl thing left her exasperated. If all went well, she thought, maybe she'd be the one to book the next treat.

'You'll love it, I'm sure,' he said, stuffing several screwed-up shirts into a small grey Samsonite.

'Why do I bother ironing anything, Colin?' she said angrily, immediately regretting being negative, as he always called her criticisms. She composed herself. 'Look, shall I do that for you? You go and make us a coffee. We've got plenty of time before we have to leave.'

He walked out of the bedroom in silence, glad, she thought, that he'd got out of doing the packing, even if it meant having to make the drinks.

When he came back his mood was better, more chipper, his excitement at the prospect of the coming Bond-fest evident on his face. 'They're you go,' he said, handing her the mug, handle-first - a first in twenty-odd years of marriage, she noted. Maybe he really was trying to change.

She gave him a smile. 'All done,' she said, waving a hand towards the two small cases on the bed.

'You got everything into one bag each?'

'You know me.'

'Did you pack -,'

'Your "Director" T-shirt, yes, that's in there.'

'And the hat?'

'Hat?'

'Yes, my Cubby Broccoli baseball cap.'

She flushed, remembering the day she'd picked it up for the umpteenth time when it had fallen out of the wardrobe and decided that it would be far more use to the charity shop than to a grown man.

'I, um, I haven't seen it. Didn't you get rid of it?'

He looked quizzical. 'Get rid of it? Why would I get rid of it? It was signed.'

She flushed again.

'Oh, by who?'

'What? Who signed a Cubby Broccoli baseball cap? Nelson Mandela, obviously.'

She hated it when he ridiculed her, hated his superior sneering face when he tried to make her look stupid, hated him at that moment. 'Oh fuck off, Colin!' she screamed and stormed out of the room, coffee slopping onto the carpet.

'Christ Mary, mind the carpet!'

'Fuck the carpet,' she shouted, from halfway down the stairs.

The bus station was busy; people passing in every direction like robots programmed to be somewhere else, no matter who, or what, got in their way.

'There it is!' he exclaimed, pointing towards a shiny white coach with dark windows. 'At least it's a nice new bus,' he said, as if this was a major consideration.

Mary lugged her case towards the vehicle, joining a small group of similarly-burdened passengers. So far, she noted with growing dread, she was the only woman. The driver stepped forward and offered to take her case, swinging it into the open compartment on the side of the bus. Colin's newly-revived chivalry hadn't extended to carrying her case for her. Besides, he had his own bag to contend with, as well as the paperwork for the trip, which he had put between his teeth in order to use both hands to haul the bag into the hold and then, curiously, left the paperwork there, so that he looked, Mary thought, like a dog bringing the mail to its master. She laughed, but only on the inside, not wanting to risk reigniting the earlier blow-up which had threatened to make them late.

Once onto the bus they were directed to their allotted seats by a smart young woman in a tight-fitting business suit with a crisp white blouse beneath. Mary noticed the fake tan, and the carefully-emphasised cleavage, and she noticed that Colin had noticed the latter feature too. Looking around before taking her seat she spotted only one other couple, younger than them; the girl pretty but heavily made up and her partner smart but casual in a brown waxed jacket and round-necked sweater. How like her and Colin they were at that age, she thought, giggling together over a shared joke, and how things had changed. His moods, the drinking, the explosive temper and the way that, where once he had looked her up and down, now he seemed to look straight through her.

When all the passengers were seated, Becky (as the buxom tour guide had introduced herself) launched into a well-rehearsed and rather patronising greeting, heavily geared, Mary felt, towards the predominantly male audience. If she'd had reservations about agreeing to come on this trip, her worst fears were being realised. It seemed that they were to start the tour by driving, via central London, to Pinewood Studios in Buckinghamshire. Along the way, Becky assured them, she would be pointing out various locations which the more astute amongst them would no doubt recognise and then be able to identify in which Bond movie, or indeed book, they had appeared.

Mary had already come to the conclusion that the majority of her travelling companions - Colin included - were unlikely to have actually read any of Ian Fleming's writing and would almost certainly be relying only on their knowledge of the various films. To Mary's growing horror Becky had then turned this exercise into a competition, the passengers being encouraged to shout out the name of the movie in which the location had featured as soon as they recognised it. There would be a prize for the most knowledgeable fan. Colin seemed buoyed by the prospect of competing with his fellow devotees and nudged Mary.

'Spot on, this. I'm going to win for sure.'

By the time they reached Pinewood they had been invited to identify more than a dozen locations, including the old MI6 building in Whitehall (Dr No), the new MI5 building on the South Bank (Quantum of Solace, Skyfall), "Blades", really Pratt's, club in St James's (Die Another Day), the River Thames itself (The World is Not Enough), the Houses of Parliament (almost every Bond movie) and Royal Ascot (A View to a Kill). Colin had only managed to shout out two of them before anyone else, and his mood had thus darkened. The prize, when it came, did little to help; a signed Cubby Broccoli baseball cap which went to a rather overweight man with a South-London accent and, it seemed, a worryingly encyclopaedic knowledge of movie locations.

Things improved for Mary at Pinewood. There was a rather lovely cafeteria bedecked, unsurprisingly, with photographs of a whole plethora of film stars. There were pictures of the various Bonds of course but for Mary these were completely overshadowed by amazing monochrome shots of the likes of Audrey Hepburn, Virginia McKenna,

Dirk Bogarde, Vanessa Redgrave and - her favourite - Mia Farrow, her wistful beauty highlighted by the black and white format and the stylish, glamorous dress from the set of The Great Gatsby. The later, colour pictures of various actors were, she thought, less endearing, particularly the inevitable scantily-clad Bond girls whose images seemed to leap out as if mocking her. Mary was happy to spend some time here though, but Colin was keen to move on.

'Just a slice of cake and a coffee then,' he'd agreed when Mary had first pointed out the refreshments. 'Don't want to miss anything.'

They sat in near-silence whilst consuming their meagre snack, Colin poring over the guidebook they'd been handed upon arrival.

'Look,' he'd occasionally chirp, before highlighting something that had excited him, 'they've still got the submarines from Skyfall!'

Mary steeled herself. 'Perhaps,' she began, 'you'd prefer to go 'round on your own?'

Colin looked angry. 'Well, if you're going to be a miserable killjoy all day then I may as well be on my own.' He stood up and stomped off, clutching the guidebook, only to turn around a few seconds later and return. 'I need the camera,' he mumbled.

Mary smiled. 'Here you go,' she said, handing it to him, 'and don't take too many, you'll need space on the memory card for dinner tonight and Brussels tomorrow.'

Colin walked off to find the rest of the group, leaving Mary alone, stirring the cream into her cappuccino.

'Is this seat taken?'

She recognised him straight away, of course. She'd only been looking at his photograph five minutes before, and there was the time when two of her girlfriends had once dragged her along to see Mamma Mia.

'Um, yes, I mean, no, please.' She indicated towards the empty chair opposite.

'It gets so busy in here, especially when there's a big movie in production. Are you in this one?'

'What? Me? Oh no, no, I'm just, well, I'm just here with my husband - he's on the Bond Locations Tour.'

'Aah, I see.'

She noticed his perfect complexion, the way his face creased as he smiled, how his eyes seemed to be an impossible shade of the deepest blue and his voice, oh, that voice!

'Don't worry,' she said, 'I think they're all a bunch of losers if I'm frank. I only agreed to come on it because...' she faltered.

He smiled again. 'I'm supposed to be doing what they call a "meet and greet" with them in half an hour. Frankly I'm dreading it. I mean, what am I supposed to say?'

Mary laughed. 'I can't believe that you, of all people, are lost for words!'

'Well, you know what they say, without a script...'

Mary went back to stirring and then said, 'You know, sometimes I think that's what my life is like; a script that I've got to stick to, never get my lines wrong, never ad lib.' She looked up at him and he returned her stare.

After a moment he said, 'You know what?' Maybe it's time for a rewrite.'

Colin was in the group just inside the open doors of a large hangar. Behind them stood the scaffolding and mocked-up panels of two enormous fake submarines. Becky had gathered them together for a surprise. There was a ripple of excitement at the distinctive sound of an Aston Martin V12 engine as it rumbled towards them. Then suddenly it was there, right in front of them: James Bond's car! Some gasped and, as it slewed to a halt, there was a flurry of clicking shutters and flashes. Brosnan flicked open the driver's door and stepped out.

'Good afternoon,' he said, casually perching on the front wing, 'it's nice to see you all today, and thanks for coming. Now, has anyone got any questions for me?'

A few people responded: Did he miss playing Bond? Did he do his own stunts? How much did he get paid? He answered each in turn with polished politeness.

Finally one person put up their hand.

'You have a question?'

'Er, yes. Who's that in the car?'

In all the excitement no one had noticed that there was anyone else in the car. Now all eyes turned towards the figure reclining in the leather passenger seat.

'Mary?' Colin's mouth drooped open like a fish.

'Well, I'd better be off,' said the star, sliding back into the driving seat, 'nice to meet you all.'

A screech of tyres and a cloud of acrid smoke signalled the rapid departure of the Aston. Everyone stood in silence, not sure exactly what they had just seen.

Finally, a fat man with a South-London accent and wearing a signed Cubby Broccoli baseball cap turned to Colin and said, 'Ere, mate, do you know 'er?'

Colin was silent for a moment, and then he said,

'Yes, I do. She's my Bond girl.'

One Person in the Crowd

Carol Hyde

They call me the Angel of Death, or the Grim Reaper, but I don't deserve either of these titles. Despite my many incarnations, I have not yet reached the exulted status of Angel. And nothing about what I do is remotely grim. Just as a midwife assists babies into the world, so I assist souls to transfer back to their eternal home. And just as there is much joy at the arrival of a wanted baby, so there is even more joy when a soul returns to eternity. It is not for me to choose who will die, any more than it is the midwife who chooses which soul will be born anew. The idea of me as a black robed skeleton, holding a scythe, never ceases to amuse me. Why would I need a scythe? My role is to raise up, not cut down.

Right now, I am hovering over a large busy beach. Very soon, one person in this crowd will die. It is my role to find that soul and welcome it back home, where it will prepare for its next incarnation. Death can come at any moment, to any one of the bodies below me, without warning. Right now, there are twenty five people here with cancer. Only eight of them are aware of their illness, the remainder will learn of their condition over the coming months. Fifteen of them will survive the disease, but none of them will die today.

Up ahead, I see a small child, choking. Her parents are frantically patting her back and putting their fingers down her throat. People around them offer advice, but feel helpless. The child loses consciousness, her lips turn blue. A nearby nurse sees the commotion and comes to help. She wraps her arms around the child to apply the Heimlich manoeuver. Once, nothing. Twice… nothing. Then suddenly the child's throat clears, she gulps in air, opens her eyes, and begins to cry. She will die another day. In fact, according to my records, this little one has a very interesting life ahead of her, full of choices and opportunities to learn and advance.

I move on and see a decrepit old man named George, whom I recognize as the soul Malia. In this current life, he has never hurt another person, but he has never done any obvious good, either. He chose to be born the unwanted only child of a wealthy couple who abandoned him on his fifth birthday by dying in a car accident. From then, until the age of eighteen, he was a ward of the state. On reaching legal age, he was released into the world with plenty of money, but few social skills. He has lived the life of a recluse, in the same house all his life, spending little of his money. He has never married nor had children. He has never given or received love. Nor has he ever given or received a gift. Although his health is failing, he has given no consideration to whom he will leave his estate, and he has no will.

All his life he has had choices – whether to reach out to people or avoid them; to seek a mate or remain alone; to give or withhold. Did he make the right choices? It's not for me to judge. But he has had a profound effect on the few people he couldn't avoid – his neighbours, shopkeepers and other business people. His lifestyle confuses them, and they make assumptions about him which are rarely right. They shake their heads and wonder why he hasn't made an effort to enjoy life. They've learned that money isn't the secret to happiness, and promise themselves to live their lives to the full. So perhaps, in his own way, he has enriched their lives which may yet leave an impression on generations to come. I'll come back for George in a couple of years, for he still has more choices to make.

Further along the beach, a young woman is screaming for help. She and her new young husband have travelled here from Japan for their honeymoon. Her husband is struggling in a rip which is quickly washing him away from the shore. A crowd gathers and watches him frantically waving for help before disappearing below the waves. Each time he reappears it seems more difficult for him to keep his face above the water.

The lifesavers see him and launch the surf ski, but it's several minutes before they reach him. When they do, he is no longer struggling but sinking. One of the lifesavers dives down to retrieve his limp body. Back on the beach they fight to revive him, but it's too late. All they can do is try to comfort the young bride, who still expects her husband to open his eyes.

Toshiko is beside me now, looking down on the scene. He can't help but feel his wife's pain and desperation. I remind him his death was pre-ordained by them both, before they were born, but he ignores me. He wants to remain with his soul mate on the beach. I tell him his death is a gift to this lovely young woman, because he is giving her an opportunity to grow and learn through her pain and loss.

He stares at me incredulously, then hesitates. Recognition is dawning. He is remembering who he really is. He looks back at his young wife with so much love and yearning, then relaxes as he accepts the separation. He knows she will be all right, that her life in this world will unfold as it should. And he knows they will be reunited. An earthly lifetime is a blink of the eye in eternity. He turns and smiles at me, and together we return home.

On His Majesty's Secret Service

Susan Morley

One of my father's prisoner-of-war letters intrigues me.

Although it is written on an air mail form in pencil just like all the others, it's addressed to a Mrs Campbell, at the *Hotel do Parque*, Estoril, Portugal.

The postmark is 16th December 1940. A pink sticker states that the letter has been opened by a censor. As usual, Dad has written his name on the back, his prisoner-of-war number and printed underneath is the name of the first prison he was sent to Oflag V11C.

Amongst the bundle of air letters and postcards Dad gave me I find the pen and ink sketch on the 1940 Christmas card of the prison's façade. It shows an entrance-way to an imposing fortress of a castle with slit windows, and thick stone walls. It looks a formidable place, and yet I remember Dad telling me, 'I could go for walks with one of my captors in the early days. We'd go out into the surrounding countryside. We often talked at length in English about books and medicine. It was all very civil.'

When I check the air letters that I have there are three that pre-date this one to Estoril. Two were posted on the 18th September and the 20th November to his eldest sister, Kathleen, in Belfast along with the Christmas card. One was sent to his mother on 16th November 1940 in Monaghan.

In the first letter to his sister he tells her he's been a prisoner for three months in Southern Germany. He says that he can see The Alps in the distance, and that he's asked his mother to send a parcel of food containing tinned meat, fish, butter, chocolate, and cigarettes. He stresses that 'parcels are restricted to a weight of 10 lbs.'

In his second letter to Kathleen, he mentions three Irish men, two of whom he says are with him at Oflag V11C, and a third by the name of Madden is also in Germany. I wonder if he wants Kathleen to let someone in Belfast know of these men's whereabouts.

In the letter to his mother, he thanks her for her last two letters, and says that as yet he hasn't received any of the parcels that she's sent.

On this mysterious letter to neutral Portugal my father's pencil address has been crossed through with blue ink, I assume by the recipient, and his mother's name and address in Southern Ireland written in a flowing style over the top. The second postmark is dated the 2nd January 1941 from Estoril, seventeen days after the letter was posted from Germany.

Inside he writes: DeaR MRS CAMPBELL, Please forward this letter to MRS POLLOCK, KnockacoNNy Hse, MONAGHAN, IRELAND.

It seems strange that Dad has interspersed capitals with lower case letters, almost as though it's been done deliberately.

The date at the top is 9.12.40.

'Dear Mamma, So far I have had 4 letters from home but no parcels yet. Please send my letters by aiRmail.'

He seems to have difficulty writing anything other than a capital R. He then explains that he doesn't wish her to send any food parcels as he believes the Red Cross will 'soon have that well in hand.' This contradicts what he has written to his sister asking to be sent various items of food. He says that he is 'waiting every day for the clothes paRcel to aRRive,' because his present stock is low and almost worn out.

In the earlier letters he hasn't mentioned that he needs any clothes!

He tells her that he is still working in the sick room, but 'unfoRtunately I can't send you a pResent – probably next Xmas 1941.'

Why has he sent this letter via Mrs. Campbell in Portugal asking her to forward it home when his mother already knows his whereabouts? He must have an ulterior motive. I want to know who this Mrs. Campbell is, and more about the hotel where the letter has been sent.

Thank heavens for Google.

As soon as I type in the *Hotel do Parque*, I discover it was The Headquarters for Nazi spies and their axis allies during the war. This troubles me. Why is my father writing to someone with a Scottish surname at an hotel in Estoril renown for German spies?

I'm surprised too that the letter arrived. Surely the German censor must have known what was going on in Portugal. Why didn't he intercept it?

I try to find out as much as I can. I want to know what the hotel looked like, but I can't find a single picture of the exterior, only one taken inside where a chess champion by the name of Alekhine died in his room slumped in a chair, sitting in front of a table with his dinner half-eaten in front of him wrapped in his overcoat. The photograph, taken after he was discovered, makes his death look very suspicious. Had he been poisoned?

A headline states that the post mortem revealed he died of a heart attack. The year is 1946.

I wonder how many unexplained deaths may have occurred at this hotel after I come across an interview given by The Head Concierge, Antonio Pinto about what it was like to work there during the war.

'Occasionally occupants disappeared. One couldn't be sure that they hadn't been kidnapped or had slipped away quietly to lie low. The porters would simply collect all their belongings and leave them labelled and packaged in a storeroom.'

I imagine a small room crammed with all those unclaimed possessions. Perhaps some of the disappeared left expensive personal items or weapons behind.

I find an article that describes the lengths that both the Allies and Germans would go to – to try and fool one another. It seems the British tried to plant an agent who spoke fluent German inside the hotel carrying clothes from Hamburg, and false papers, but when he went to lie down in his room he found a union jack, and an Eton school tie under the covers.

I finally manage to find a black and white picture on flickr of the hotel's graceful Art Deco exterior. It buoys me up and makes me think about visiting the place where Dad sent this mysterious letter. But my exhilaration doesn't last long. On further reading I discover the hotel is long gone. Apparently when it was torn down, after the war, hundreds of bugging devices, and a maze of wires were found hidden within its walls.

My research tells me that M15, M16 and M19 were all involved in Portugal during The Second World War as were SOE (Special Operations Executive).

Portugal was the country where displaced Royalty fled along with wealthy Jews desperate to escape. It was a place of transit where many people were waiting for papers to take them to The United States or Palestine. There were daily flights between Lisbon and Bristol until flight 777 was shot down in 1943 by The Germans who mistakenly thought Churchill was on board.

While some made Lisbon, the capital, their base, the seaside resort of Estoril was far more inviting for those who wanted the chance to unwind.

The *Palacio Hotel* in Estoril was favoured by Royalty and by the famous for its seclusion and the distractions it offered with its adjacent Casino. Both buildings were close to the *Hotel do Parque*, and another hotel the *Atlantico*, also favoured by German spies, and like the *Parque* knocked down after the war. The three hotels were in close proximity to one another in a square within which was a palm-treed park.

The *Palacio* still stands. It is a most elegant looking place built in 1930 in the grand style of the architecture of Biarritz. It sits in manicured lawns that face out to sea. During the war it was The Allies Headquarters. It was where Ian Fleming, the British Naval Intelligence

Officer, stayed in 1941 when he was sent to manage a Yugoslavian double agent. Popov was being paid for feeding misinformation to the Germans whom he loathed whilst working for the British for nothing. Fleming would meet him regularly in the wood-panelled bar where Popov preferred his martini to be shaken rather than stirred.

It seems more than mere coincidence that The British Ambassador to Portugal's surname at the time happened to be Campbell. But, I'm puzzled as to why my father sent the letter to the *Hotel do Parque* rather than the *Palacio*. Was it a ruse so that the German censors might not suspect his motives? Maybe his choice of destination was regarded as less suspicious. But how would the British Ambassador have been able to receive mail sent to an hotel full of Nazi spies?

Could Campbell have had an arrangement with a member of staff to intercept letters sent to 'his wife'?

I find a photo of Sir Ronald Hugh Campbell. He looks suave and very much the diplomat in a dark suit sitting at a table discussing matters with another man.

I wonder how my father knew of him. It seems unlikely that they could ever have met. By the time of the mystery letter's arrival, Campbell had only recently taken up his post in November 1940 following the fall of France. He had been The British Ambassador in Paris beforehand.

I picture him reading this very letter. It has survived for almost seventy-five years; the pencil and the ink still legible, on the almost transparent paper. I imagine Campbell sitting alone on an elegant chair at a desk piled high with papers reading and re-reading it before passing it on to one of the secret services.

I wonder what he thought about an Irish doctor offering to spy from his German prison.

Perhaps it was the perfect cover.

Once my father's captors discovered he was Irish he told us, 'Their attitude changed.' It didn't take long before he was singled out for special treatment, taken to a house where he was plied with food and luxuries while they tried to persuade him to defect. They wanted him to join William Joyce, Lord Haw Haw, in Berlin, to assist with his radio broadcasts.

When my father refused he was sent to work in an underground hospital.

'It was grim. I didn't see the light of day for some time.'

Then he was sent to Oflag V11C, Laufen Castle, in Bavaria where he was imprisoned with other officers from The Army and The RAF.

My doctor father locked up with men desperate to escape must have felt compelled to remain; unable to contemplate a home run as long as he was needed to care for the sick. He always intimated that to be captured so early on was most humiliating, but having a job to do was his salvation. Perhaps engaging in espionage within the camps helped his morale while he had to wait out the war.

The spy who loved us never bragged, and rarely spoke about what he had to endure. It was Mum who sometimes let things slip. 'Your father was far more adventurous than he's ever let on. He was up to all sorts risking life and limb by spying and sending coded messages.'

Sometimes she teased him about his, 'so-called girlfriends dotted around Europe.' She used to say, 'Before I met your father he was quite the ladies' man. Heaven knows how he found the time to keep in touch with so many.'

As an officer he was only allowed to write three letters and four postcards a month. But maybe there wasn't a limit on the number of letters he could receive.

I wonder what his family made of his subterfuge. My grandmother must have been worried sick knowing that her only son was prepared to put his life at risk.

I wish I could know what my grandfather thought. The fact that he isn't ever addressed or mentioned in a single letter speaks volumes.

Once Dad confessed, 'I thought my time was up. We were shoved into the back of a truck and driven away from the camp then forced to get out. A gun was aimed at my head.'

'What did you do?'

'I pleaded for my life and said if you shoot any of us you're contravening the Geneva Convention. '

I think Dad could see how shocked I was because he said, 'It was stupid to have tried to reason my way out, but when you're staring death in the face you have nothing to lose.'

He never elaborated on why the incident happened. I assumed it was for doing something to help someone escape. I know he helped several people who were desperate for a way out.

I want to find out about how the codes worked. There must have been a formula.

Very few articles have been written on the subject so far, but I'm heartened by a recent one in a newspaper that states the Maths Department of Plymouth University helped the relatives of a Naval Officer crack his secret code. Perhaps I should write to them.

The only concrete evidence that I have is contained within Dad's letters of which there are only fifteen. I read each one carefully looking for discrepancies.

There are four strange mentions in four separate letters. In one to his mother written on 17/12/41 he finishes by saying, 'It would have been betteR if you had converted The Manwell fund into cigaRettes. HoweveR I have wRitten to him twice.'

In the next letter that I have to her dated 7/2/42 he states, 'I have not had your June paRcel or any from Tom Manwell for a long time so I take it we may give them up foR lost.'

And in the following letter dated 14/2/42 he mentions Tom Manwell again when he says, 'I have not had any reply to my letter to Tom Manwell. Was soRRy to hear about MRS GRay.'

The fourth strange comment is in his letter to his mother dated 22/7/42 in which he says he has had a letter, 'fRom a friend in PoRtugal who sends me odd paRcels of saRdines etc.'

My one regret is that I didn't unearth any of these discrepancies while Dad was still alive.

If only I'd read his prisoner-of-war letters when they were first handed to me in 1993 before I passed them to him. I'd have been able to ask why he sent the letter via Mrs Campbell in Portugal, who the friend was from there who sent parcels of sardines, whether there really was a Tom Manwell and what the fund was, if the capital Rs in the middle of words were important to the code, and how it could be deciphered.

Here and Now

Valerie Moffit

Ellie feels sorry that Newcastle's buses aren't yellow any more. The Corporation colour used to be so cheering on the grey streets. Now – since deregulation, she supposes – the rival bus companies compete for road space in liveries of dull red and duller blue. They add no cheer at all.

She is on her way to visit Kirsten and Mark, old friends from student days.

'They're organising a 40th reunion for our year,' Kirsten told Ellie on the phone last month. 'Shall I put you on the list? It might be fun. And you can stay with us.'

Ellie heard herself say yes, that would be nice, and regretted her haste as soon as she'd put the phone down. Kirsten emailed her with details of the weekend – talks in the archaeology department; a guided tour of the newly refurbished museum of antiquities; a formal dinner on Saturday evening – and she felt even more downcast. But she told herself it would be good to see the old place again, and so she booked her train ticket from King's Cross.

As students, she and Kirsten had joined the University's archery club, partly because it was an opportunity to learn a traditional skill that chimed with their interest in medieval history; but mainly because they reckoned that it would be a good way to meet men. Sure enough, Kirsten had met Mark and they had soon become a couple. After graduating, they had married and settled in the city. Ellie hadn't seen them since their daughters were small, and now they were grandparents. It was alarming how much time had passed.

They've told her to catch the number 26 from Eldon Square - so here she is, sharing a bus shelter with half a dozen other hopefuls, backs turned to the blowing drizzle and eyes scanning the busy street. It's June, but Ellie recalls that in the North East it's best not to expect sunny weather; then, if the clouds clear, it's a bonus. The number 26 arrives at last and she climbs aboard, finding a seat next to a large man in a black and white bobble hat. No going back now. Not for the first time, she wonders if Barb will be at the reunion. But of course that's a ridiculous idea.

Barb had detested the name Barbara. And woe betide anyone who called her Babs or, worse still, Barbie. That warranted a swift kick in the testicles – on most occasions metaphorically, but at least once in reality. Ellie saw it happen.

So, Barb it was. Her hair was a mass of copper curls that she teased into an afro. She had green eyes that looked at you quizzically, as if she could see into your soul; and a lop-sided grin that suggested nothing was that serious – lighten up! Velvet flares clothed her long legs, and her favourite Indian shirt was decorated with tiny mirrors. The smell of patchouli hung around her: exotic, disturbing. Secretly, Ellie might have been a little in love with her. Perhaps more than a little.

Barb scarcely acknowledged most of the male students they saw on a daily basis, and indeed they were generally a sorry, spotty lot. Ellie made do with them as occasional boyfriends, but the men Barb preferred were older postgraduates and usually belonged to CND or the Socialist Workers' Party. Ellie would go along to meetings, hoping to be accepted as a comrade, but she knew she was just one of the hangers-on. Barb was always in the midst of the action, organising protests in the students' union or sit-ins at the registry. After a while Ellie noticed that Barb had abandoned her 'love them and leave them' routine and had somehow settled on one man. This was Frank, a charismatic type who held the floor, inspiring the foot-soldiers with his furious rhetoric.

To be honest, Ellie didn't understand why Barb fancied him. He wasn't tall - in fact only an inch or so taller than Barb – and his dark blond hair was scraped into a pony tail. He had acne scars on his cheek. But when he played guitar and sang his angry songs, you could see that people – both men and women - took notice.

'This is Ellie,' Barb said to him one evening. 'She's doing archaeology.'

'Is that so?' Frank raised an eyebrow and looked amused.

'She's coming on the march next week, aren't you, Ellie?'

Ellie nodded.

'Good for you,' he said, and turned away. Ellie felt she had been dismissed.

'Scuse me pet,' rumbles the man in the bobble hat, 'it's my stop.'

'Oh, sorry.' Ellie stands to let him out and then slides along the seat to take the well-warmed spot by the window. There is still some way to go before Kirsten and Mark's street, and she allows herself to sink back into her daydream.

On the march they brandished placards that proclaimed:

MRS THATCHER, MILK SNATCHER!

Barb led the chanting and singing. It was exhilarating, inspiring. Ellie felt as though they could change boring old Britain; that young people with new ideas would sweep away the old grey men that ran the country. Everyone was so optimistic. As for Margaret Thatcher, she might have been a snooty version of Ellie's own mother. She'd just been put in charge of education, and her plan was to save the Government money by doing away with free school milk for primary school children. Unbelievable.

That evening there'd been a Geog Soc disco in the Claremont Tower, and Ellie and Barb had danced like creatures possessed, swooping and leaping around the floor to All Right Now, circling each other in a mad, drunken delirium. Frank sat at a corner table with his mates, nursing a pint and reviewing the day's protest. After a while he called Barb over with a jerk of his head.

She came back to Ellie and collected her Afghan coat.

'Gotta go', she said. 'See you next week.'

'Oh - yeah. Right.' As Barb left, Ellie felt the energy in the room go with her.

Gazing through the dirty window of the bus, Ellie's eyes fill with tears. She brushes them away. How stupid to be upset at something that happened so long ago. But she didn't see Barb the next week, or even the one after that. Ellie's mind drifts back to a Saturday morning almost three weeks after the disco.

She was in bed, slowly emerging from the depths of sleep. She'd been swimming in deep water, except that she couldn't swim and no-one could hear her shout. Someone was snoring like a pig, and an extra loud snort startled her awake. There was no-one else in the room. She stumbled over to the wash basin and splashed her face with cold water, stuck her tongue out at the mirror. What a wreck. Memories of the previous evening slowly bobbed to the surface. She had thrown up behind a bus shelter. And at some point she had fallen in a hedge; there were scratches on her arms to prove it. Sal and Jacky had pulled her out. They'd all had a hilarious time.

But there'd been something wrong. Oh, of course. Barb wasn't there. It wasn't like her to miss the regular Friday night pub crawl, and that was the second week in a row that she'd not shown up. Ellie saw some of her mates from Sociology and they said she hadn't been to lectures for a while. What's more, Barb was a regular fixture in the union sandwich bar, and it felt like ages since she and Ellie had met there for cheese and pickle rolls and frothy coffee.

A plan of action began to form in Ellie's muzzy head. She would go round to Barb's flat and see what was up. Maybe she'd got the flu. A visit would cheer her up, and Ellie could offer to do some shopping. This was a good plan. But first, a cooked breakfast. She was ravenous.

After double eggs and bacon and a stack of fried bread, she felt restored and caught the number 33 round to Barb's flat. She rang the bell; no reply. But she could hear Janis Joplin wailing, at full volume, 'Take another little piece of my heart now, baby ...' so she knew Barb was there. After a while one of her housemates opened the front door and Ellie set off up the stairs to her room in the attic. Janis's raucous wail got louder as she climbed. She knocked on the door and, when there was no answer, she went in. Barb was sitting on the floor, eyes closed, her back against the bed. Beside her was an almost empty bottle of Jack Daniel's and an ashtray overflowing with fag ends.

Ellie stepped across the room and lifted the pick-up off the record. Silence. Barb opened her eyes. They were bloodshot and there was an angry bruise on her right cheekbone.

'Hi Ellie,' she slurred.

Ellie knelt down next to her. 'You look dreadful,' she said.

'Thanks, kid,' said Barb with a hint of her old smile. 'Not feeling too good.'

'What happened here?' Ellie reached out to touch Barb's face, but she flinched away.

'Oh, me and Frank got into a bit of an argument, I s'pose. Don't worry, I gave him a pop too.'

'Where is he?'

'Dunno. Haven't seen him for a while.' Barb put her head back and closed her eyes.

Ellie made a decision. 'Look, why don't you go and have a shower, and I'll make some coffee?'

To her surprise, Barb said 'Okey doke,' and got unsteadily to her feet.

In the here and now, Ellie thinks, she would get Barb out of there, and she'd report Frank to the police. But back then, it had never occurred to them. They were just girls, and students at that. If they'd been bold or foolish enough to go to the police station, the duty sergeant would have laughed in their faces and told Barb to behave herself and stop annoying her boyfriend.

Back then, what she did was help Barb to the bathroom, clean up her room a bit and make her a mug of good strong Nescaff. She didn't ask her what the argument with Frank was about; she didn't want to pry. And Barb didn't volunteer any more information.

Arriving at Kirsten and Mark's, Ellie presents them with the bottle of Merlot that she bought at King's Cross, and she knows they'll have plenty more. After shepherd's pie and raspberry pavlova, she and Kirsten leave Mark with the pot washing, as he calls it, and continue chatting companionably over a third bottle of wine.

'I was thinking about Barb today,' says Ellie. 'You don't think she'll be at the reunion, do you?'

'God, no!' says Kirsten. 'She couldn't leave Newcastle fast enough. And as far as I know, she hasn't been back.'

'Ah.'

'Last I heard, she was living in France.'

Ellie says, 'I was wondering what happened to her and Frank. Do you know?'

'Ah, Frank!' Kirsten turns down her mouth. 'That nasty little Trot. Mark used to call him our pocket-size Tariq Ali.'

Ellie remembers that Kirsten had always been rather conservative - a policeman's daughter. But she nods.

'Mmm. It's funny, isn't it – peculiar, I mean - how those left-wing men tended to be horrible to their women?'

'Yes; they were all for workers' rights, but women's rights didn't figure in their calculations. They thought feminism was a side issue, if they thought about it at all.'

Ellie, emboldened by the wine, decides to confide in Kirsten.

'I think Frank beat her up, once, when they had a big row.'

'Oh, I'm not surprised,' says Kirsten. 'That would have been over the baby.'

Ellie feels a constriction in her throat and can't trust herself to speak.

'Didn't you know?' says Kirsten. 'Barb got pregnant in our last term. That's why she dropped out and never took her final exams.'

Ellie lets this forty-year-old information sink in.

'Frank wanted her to have an abortion, of course,' continues Kirsten. 'That's what they fell out about. God, he was such a shit.'

'And did she …?'

'Have the baby? Yes, but she gave it up for adoption.'

'Oh.' Ellie doesn't know what to say.

'I'm sorry, Ellie,' says Kirsten. 'I didn't mean to shock you. I thought you knew.'

Ellie thinks, I loved her, but she didn't trust me with her secret.

She tells Kirsten, 'No, I never knew Barb was pregnant. But then, we weren't all that close.'

It's in the Tea Leaves

Jo Gamgee

Elizabeth was on the telephone in the hall, holding a letter in her hand.

'Oh, good, thanks for that, Ed. I'll be there at four.' She paused. 'I'll tell you when I see you. Bye.' She replaced the receiver, checked her bag for handkerchief, money, glasses, powder, lipstick, comb, book, keys, and set off for the bus stop. Even half an hour face to face would be better than discussing it over the telephone.

They had arranged to meet in Lyons Corner House near Russell Square, where Edward worked as an architect. He was often able to take time out of the office in the middle of the day. The bus from south London to town was slow and her mind was unsettled as she looked out of the window. People in the streets were going about their business, enjoying the bright May sunshine. It was hard to believe there was a war on. She jumped off the bus at the traffic lights and ran to meet him. She was late, again. He was sitting at a table by the window, reading the newspaper.

'Oh, Ed, I'm sorry I'm late. It's horrible to be at the mercy of the buses. It just crawled along.'

He stood up, smiled and kissed her on the cheek. 'Never mind, you're here now. Tea?'

'Yes, please. A strong one.' She sat down opposite him with a sense of pride. He was tall, casually dressed, relaxed and confident and she liked his courteous way with the waitress who served them. Leaving the letter on the table for him to read, she made her way to the cloakroom to check her hair, powder her nose and touch up her lipstick.

By the time she returned there was tea for two and a cake for her. Edward was smiling as he spoke. 'Congratulations, darling. I'm not surprised. They are lucky to have you.'

'And now I don't know what to do.' There he sat, just watching and listening. 'It seemed a good idea when I applied,' she went on. 'To work out of London, I mean. But now I'm not so sure. I was even homesick when I went to Germany on that school exchange. We were only away for three weeks.'

'When do they want you to start?'

'September. Until July. Then I'll be qualified and can teach anywhere I want.' She waited for his reaction. 'What do you think I should do?'

'Teaching was always your plan, wasn't it?'

'Yes.'

'And it makes sense to be out of London.'

'Because of the bombing, you mean?'

'Yes. You want to work, don't you?' He looked at her intently. 'Clever women do, I always thought.'

'But a girls' boarding school? And why did I ever think it was a good idea to go to Devon?'

'It's not for long. We'll write.' He looked pleased. 'And we can have long holidays together.'

Elizabeth smiled back, took a sip of lukewarm tea, then spoke again. 'I have a feeling of dread. I won't be happy there.'

'What would make you happy? I've always wondered.' He asked it simply enough, but there was something in his look which made her think carefully before answering.

'The war has changed things. I long now for a house in the country, filled with love and laughter… married with children, dogs, freedom to write, read, paint, teach the piano, grow runner beans.' She looked down. 'All this when there's a war on. It's story book stuff.'

'These are not trivial aspirations.' He hesitated, but only for a moment. 'You're beautiful and I love you.' His eyes were shining. 'You can have what you want.' He held her gaze. 'We can have what we want.'

The next day Mary, a student nurse at Camberwell Hospital, responded, as best friends do, to an urgent request to meet. She put the piece of cake that was on its way towards her mouth back down on the plate.

'He asked you just like that?'

'Yes.'

'On one knee?' Mary bit into the cake.

'No. He just said, "Let's get married".'

'And?'

'I wasn't expecting it, even though we've been together for ages. He wants it and he really loves me.' Lizzie tried to read her friend's expression. 'You like him, don't you?'

'Yes, I do. You've known him for ages and you seem good together. I agree he's special. Not everyone has an MG at twenty-four.'

'That sounds horrible. It's not about the money.'

'Do you love him?'

Lizzie knew it would be fatal to hesitate. 'Yes, I do. And it's important to me that he's a pacifist. You know how I feel about that. But am I ready to be married?'

'I've got to go, Lizzie. I'm back on duty in ten minutes. Promise me you will not rush into anything.'

'But he deserves an answer.'

'Why not take the job and see how you feel when you get back? He'll wait for you.'

'Wise words. Thanks, Mary.'

It was all arranged in a matter of weeks. Elizabeth took the job, accepted Edward's proposal and they told both sets of parents. At the end of May Edward set off for the Lake District, where he was staying at a Pacifist Response Gathering for a month.

'We'll look for an engagement ring when I get back,' he promised.

On the 1st of June 1941 Elizabeth was on her way to central London with a spring in her step. It is natural to leave home, start work, and plan married life, she reasoned to herself. This is the beginning of adult life. Free from indecision, she was slightly excited and smiling inwardly.

It was summer and she enjoyed wearing her favourite khaki and cream cotton frock with bare legs and flat leather sandals. Her dark brown hair, permed on the ends, lay with pleasing bounce on her shoulders. As well as the usual items, her bag contained a small bottle of 47/11 eau de cologne, notebook and pencil. She would manage without her glasses.

The meeting was held in the garden of one of the large terraced houses in the Square. The placard outside read: **Peace Pledge Union Garden Party. 3 pm. All welcome.** It was half past two when she, early for once, stepped through the open gate. The garden was an expanse of lawn, surrounded by high trees in summer leaf. The borders were a jumble of roses in full bloom, regulation wartime vegetables and herbaceous perennials, packed with colour. Another world. She was welcomed by an elderly lady with hair piled high, and signed her name in the visitors' book. Immediately Elizabeth was tongue-tied. She took the glass of lemonade to a bench in the shade, where she could watch from a distance. These bouts of shyness could strike at any time. Why had she arrived early? Why had she come at all? She dabbed her wrists and neck with a touch of eau de cologne and breathed in the reviving scent. About thirty people were gathering in the garden and they were all a blur. She smiled and made small talk when approached but stayed apart, out of the glare. Voices were becoming more animated, laughter broke out and there was a flurry of activity at the arrival of a young man, whom everybody seemed to know. She was watching from her bench, when Harry, for that was the name was on everyone's lips, emerged from the blur.

'Thank you for coming. Are you Elizabeth?'

'Yes.'

'I'm Harry.'

'Yes. I heard you arrive.' He approached her with energy in his movements, clearly exhilarated by the day. But when he sat on the bench beside her, he fell silent, waiting for her to speak. So she did. 'I'm not politically minded. I'm here to find out about things. You know; reasons, arguments.'

His response was unhurried and generous, as if in response to her diffidence. 'I'm sure you have your own reasons and arguments, instinctive ones.' He was entranced, breathing in her fragrance.

'It seems obvious to me that some people are not able to kill.' Obvious perhaps, but Elizabeth instinctively wanted to say it.

Harry nodded. 'It's a matter of individual conscience. Are we right to trust political pronouncements, what the papers say and utterances from the pulpit?' She said nothing, so he continued. 'That's what I have to argue. At a tribunal. I have been out today practising my responses.'

She was taken aback. 'Rehearsing them, do you mean?'

'Yes. They try to catch you out. They are lawyers. If all goes well, I'll get three months in the Scrubs.'

'Religious grounds are admissible, aren't they?' Elizabeth knew this from Edward. 'And we have been warned by those who were there. All that poetry.'

Harry had heard this many times. 'They say this war is different. But all wars are different. The truth comes out only years later.' Harry stood up. 'There's to be a group photograph. We are short on beauty. Please join us.'

She laughed and shook her head. 'Oh, no. I'm not sure I want to be a member of this club. I'm decidedly undecided.' How ridiculous that sounded.

Ten minutes later she was in the photograph, sitting on the grass in the front row.

When the meeting broke up Harry found her again and took her hand, 'Let's meet tomorrow. There's lots to talk about. Say a time and place.' He did not let it go until she had answered. She hesitated, averted her eyes and eventually nodded acquiescence, leaving the time and place to him. 'Good,' he said, stepping clumsily into a rose bush as he turned to go.

Blood and thorns. Elizabeth laughed, took a safety pin from the hem of her dress and carefully removed the thorns from his hand. Her short sightedness made her ideally suited to the task.

There followed a week of meeting, talking, arriving early, arriving late. They drank tea, her favourite, or beer, his, rode on buses, walked in the park to watch the ducks turn tail up on the Serpentine, and all with a racing pulse. Elizabeth wanted to get to know Harry and his world but was unsure why. She questioned herself as each day passed, swaying this way and that. Why was she so caught up in this? Why now, when good, kind, absent Edward had, without hesitation, offered her all she had said she wanted? She trembled as the road forked before her.

By the end of the week Harry and Elizabeth had their own history. 'I was late once and you were on time once and they are the only times you remember,' he said, just for the pleasure of seeing her laugh.

Mary challenged her immediately. 'You look different,' she said, as they were catching up over tea. 'And you sound different.'

'I've never felt like this before.'

'What do your parents think?'

'That I'm happy because I'm engaged to Edward.' Elizabeth pulled a magazine out of her bag. 'I just had to show you this.' She opened it at a full page photograph of a young man in a suit, looking intently ahead. 'This is Harry.'

'How did he get into Picture Post?'

'It's an article about conscientious objectors.'

Mary went straight to the point. 'Does this change things?'

'Well, yes. And no.' Her eyes met Mary's stare. 'Don't look at me like that. Ed wants me to choose an engagement ring when he gets back from the Lakes, to make it official before I go off in September.' She dropped her eyes away from Mary's stare. 'In fact, it's far from perfect, the way it's worked out. Diamonds are for ever. I'm decidedly undecided.' That ridiculous phrase again.

There was an uncomfortable silence. Mary gathered up her things. 'Let me get this right. You have to decide between two men, neither of whom is going off to fight. Whereas I, with a ring on my finger, have to say goodbye to Sam next week. Sent abroad with the medical corps.' She stood up to leave, adding unnecessarily, 'He may not come back.'

Elizabeth was immediately on her feet and put her arms around her friend. 'I'm so sorry, Mary. How thoughtless of me.' She felt intense remorse that self-interest, an unwelcome but inevitable part of falling in love should be identified, not for the first or last time, with the cause of pacifism and divide friends and families. 'Forgive me, Mary. I'm confused.'

'You certainly are. Bye.'

Elizabeth went unhappily, but sensibly, to Devon and was homesick for she knew not what. In her small comfortless room, she wondered how anyone could decide on anything to do with love and war. She lived for letters sent and received, endured three-minute phone calls in a draughty corridor and came back a qualified teacher. Edward never bought the ring. Harry did three months in Wormwood Scrubs and then worked on the land. It had not been plain sailing. There was a disturbing incident at Paddington Station when two pacifists met the same train from Devon, armed only with their love for a beautiful woman.

On 4th August 1942 Harry and Elizabeth married in a simple register office ceremony in Hereford. Time had made her chosen path clear. 'It seems excessively self-centred to keep you for myself for ever,' said Harry, when they chose the platinum wedding ring. 'Let's see how you feel in forty years.'

In 1982 Harry and Elizabeth were retired, living in a country house in Herefordshire. Their four children, two girls and two boys, were off living their own lives. To be setting up home again, buying this and that for a rural way of life was a source of unexpected pleasure. Elizabeth wanted a besom to sweep autumn leaves from the path and they unearthed one in the village supermarket. It was pleasingly rustic, with rough twigs, expertly tied to a broom handle. 'It's just the thing. Story book stuff,' she said, smiling, then caught her breath.

'I can't wrap it,' said the woman on the checkout, 'Can you take it like that?'

'Yes, that's fine,' said Harry. 'My wife's riding home on it.'

There was time to read, paint, walk the dog and grow runner beans. On the morning of August 4th Elizabeth, the early riser, pulled the newspaper from the letterbox and made her first cup of tea of the day. Inside the tea caddy, amongst the tea leaves, was a ring. Small diamonds clustered around a central ruby. She opened the paper at the Births, Deaths and Marriages, and saw Harry's announcement. ***On 4th August 1982 Harry and Elizabeth celebrate forty years of marriage. No rubies by request.*** Then she placed a card on the mat inside the front door. In her clear teacher's hand, she had written: *Forty years. Forty more, please*. She sipped her tea and waited for their day to begin.

Gettin' Over You

Caroline Cannons

The eyes behind the dark-framed spectacles flashed like blue diamonds and were glacially cold. Jamila felt the weight of the inspection and immediately looked down, in what she hoped would be perceived as an act of contrition. The baritone tic toc of the mantel clock dominated the room. Neither Jamila nor Mary, her accomplice, dared to speak, but their anxiety was palpable.

Miss Barren moved to the bay window of her study and looked out over the opulent grounds of Fenwick Manor School for Girls.

'I'd always thought that if I'd ever married I would have children.' It was barely a whisper, and not what Jamila had expected to hear. 'However, that was not to be, and I thank God for sparing me the worry of parenthood.' Miss Barren sighed.

Jamila glanced sideways and smirked as she caught Mary's eye, who immediately looked to the floor. Jamila, however, continued to observe Miss Barren. *Why would her aunt, such a handsome and intelligent woman, choose to be incarcerated in this mausoleum of a school, when there was so much to explore in the real world?*

Without warning, Miss Barren span round. Their eyes locked. Jamila thought that she saw something resembling compassion, but any warmth soon disappeared as sentence was passed.

'You will remain in detention this Friday, and will also forfeit your place at the summer ball.'

Jamila raised her chin; a hint of defiance, perhaps, but nothing more. Mary began to cry.

'You are both extremely fortunate that I am not going to take this matter any further. This punishment will suffice. Now, stop that blubbering and get back to class.' Miss Barren flicked her hand, dismissing the miscreants, as she might swat an irritating gnat.

The girls left her study, subdued and silent.

True to her word, the senior mistress kept both girls away from the celebrations. Jamila had tried to talk her aunt round, if only for Mary, but Agnes Barren was immovable. And Jamila hadn't dared to complain to the head teacher, whose filing cabinet she had tried to prise open on her mission to steal one of the Latin A-Level papers.

Several years would pass before Jamila appreciated the lesson she had been taught – that few can be trusted to keep a secret. For it had been Mary, the look-out, who had confessed to their crime.

Twenty years later, Jamila feels only deep respect for Agnes Barren, this teacher who had provided emotional and practical support at one of the lowest points of her teenage years. For when Jamila's parents were tragically killed in a freak skiing accident, it had been Miss Barren who had travelled to Cambridge to break the news. At the end of each university term she had then provided a much needed sanctuary, which allowed Jamila to gradually rebuild her life. It was shortly after graduation that Jamila was introduced to M, and she began to see Agnes Barren in a very different light. Spinster aunt. Teacher. Mentor. And spy. No. Jamila's attendance at today's funeral is not simply a duty.

The French windows have been thrown wide open on this exceptionally hot day in early June. Jamila can hear muffled voices as people gather for the wake. The cloying fragrance of jasmine and lavender is overwhelming as she meanders from the churchyard, through the gardens and in to the oak-panelled refectory. Jamila helps herself to a glass of something resembling sweet sherry, and scans the room.

Beneath a foreboding portrait of the school's first head teacher stands the present incumbent, adorned in a ceremonial gown with its inappropriately cheerful scarlet-lined hood. She is surrounded by a group of mourners whose prosaic comments would have irritated the deceased. Jamila has no wish to join this obsequious entourage.

'In this business is much sorrow,' says a honeyed voice from behind.

Jamila swivels round on her heels and hesitates, a mere nanosecond, before recognizing her former partner-in-crime.

'Mary? Mary O'Donnell? Is it really you?

'McGarity now. But yes, it is!' beams Mary.

There is no embarrassment as they embrace, then pull away to inspect each other. And, for a moment, they are the only survivors on an island surrounded by dark seas.

'Álainn!' says Mary, drinking in the sight of Jamila. 'The passing years have certainly been kinder to you.'

Jamila hooks a stray lock of Mary's hair behind her right ear. In turn, Mary leans into Jamila's palm, then checks for the small octopus tattoo on the inside of her wrist. It is still there. She chuckles and rolls back her own cotton sleeve to reveal an identical mark. Jamila smiles.

'Seriously, though,' Mary says in a tone that indicates she cannot quite believe what she is seeing, 'what's your secret elixir? Is it love, by any chance?'

'No, certainly not!'

'The lady doth protest too much, methinks.' Mary tries and fails to elicit more information.

'So, what about you, Mary?' Jamila watches as Mary twists her wedding band around her finger.

'Widowed, which accounts for my crow's feet.' Mary squints, deepening the creases to emphasise her point, and laughs. She pulls out a crumpled photograph from inside her shoulder bag, and hands it to Jamila.

A relaxed and more youthful Mary is grinning at the camera lens. Five youngsters are gathered round her. All are smiling. She introduces each child in turn.

Jamila and Mary haven't been in touch since they waved goodbye on their final day of school in 1990; family pressure, different life choices and geographical distance had been contributory factors to the breakdown of their friendship.

Jamila notices that Mary's once dark shining hair is thinning and peppered with grey; the delicate, pale-skinned hands are now red and chapped; the sparkling green eyes, dull and bloodshot.

'Tell me about you,' Mary urges, reaching out for Jamila's hand.

Over the years Jamila has avoided suspicion by offering curt half-truths. 'Civil servant. Very boring really.'

Mary's eyes immediately light up. 'That's what He used to say.'

Jamila frowns.

'You know who,' Mary says.

Jamila continues to feign confusion. Mary looks crestfallen.

'You must remember, surely?'

Jamila breaks into a wide white grin. 'Of course I remember. But, I thought that you might have outgrown the fascination with Him by now.' She takes a sip of the amber syrup and grimaces. 'Those escapades were a lifetime ago, and they got us into a lot of trouble.'

'Jamila Bond. You were the perfect female reincarnation of 007,' says Mary, wistfully. 'You loved pretending, just as much as I did.'

Jamila wags her finger. 'And you, my dear, were my Vesper Lynd!'

Mary blushes and Jamila's belly-laugh earns the pair more stern looks. Jamila ignores the disapproving tuts.

Like a kestrel focussing in on its prey, the Head Teacher flaps her way towards them. Jamila grabs Mary's elbow. 'Come on. Let's get out of here.' Snaffling an unopened bottle and two fresh glasses from the drinks table, she pulls Mary onto the terrace and down the steps towards the pond.

They sit side by side, smoking Marlboro Lights; their bare feet dangling in the cool water of the pond. As the small fish nibble at their heels, the two women reminisce about their escapades as the pupils from hell.

Unexpectedly, Mary changes the subject. 'Poor you,' she says and drapes her arm around Jamila's neck. 'Sorry about your parents' accident. Tried to get in touch through Miss Barren. She said that you'd left no forwarding address.' Mary's accent thickens with each sip of alcohol. 'Still, Barren was a good old stick. She wrote to me you know. In Ireland. Even visited Belfast once.'

Despite the heat, Jamila shivers. 'When was that?'

'Just before I married Michael. Even came to the wedding.'

Jamila's eyes narrow. 'When, exactly?'

'Spring of 95. Why?'

Jamila tops up Mary's glass.

'Didn't know you two were in touch. That's all.' Jamila sucks on the cigarette tip, inhales and then expertly blows out three rings of smoke. The fluffy hoops trail across the pond and fade away. 'You never said how your husband died?'

'Drowned in the Irish Sea.' Mary rummages in her bag and pulls out another photograph. 'We had this one taken, just before he sailed for England.' Her eyes film over. 'A day later he drowned. Fell overboard, the eejit.' She wipes her nose, then gently shakes her head. 'Probably pissed.' A man dominates the family nest. A woman is stretching up to kiss his cheek. Children are hugging the adults' legs. They are smiling as they watch the embrace. The man is looking straight into the camera lens; master of his world. Jamila inspects the ruggedly handsome face and gasps as she recognises the twinkling eyes.

Michael McGarity had been her first assignment; MI6 had identified him as dissident paramilitary. Booked on a passage to England, it was believed that he was travelling with the intention of forming splinter groups for the organisation that called itself the True IRA. Jamila's orders were to intercept, gather information and pass it on, no matter what the cost. The man's licentious nature had made the task easy. Plying him with whiskey, she'd lured him to her cabin and the rest had been textbook entrapment. McGarity had eventually passed out, giving her the opportunity to search through his clothing. She had hastily dressed, leaving him snoring and spent, whilst she fed back the intelligence. Later, when McGarity came to find her, no-one had seen his body slip over the side, and she hadn't raised the alarm.

Jamila had been thrilled with the success of the mission, and in the intervening years hadn't given it another thought. She had never considered that this man might have had a family, let alone a wife she had known and loved, and, for the first time in her career, she feels a dent in her armour.

The church clock strikes five.

'Bejeezuz! Is that the time?' Mary struggles to her feet. 'Can you give me a lift to the airport?'

Jamila rolls an unsteady Mary into the passenger seat of her red Mini Convertible and checks on the flight details. As Mary snoozes, Jamila races through Surrey, dark eyes fixed on the road ahead, her silken jet tresses pulled back from her strained pixie face. Speed focuses her concentration and helps to blot out the past.

The last call for the 19.20 flight to Belfast is being announced as they dash through the Southern Terminal. After a swift embrace they part, each promising to keep in touch. Jamila watches on as her Nemesis is channelled through the check points. Before Mary disappears from view, she turns and waves a final farewell, just as she did twenty years previously. Jamila returns a kiss and with it a whispered apology.

The radio blasts out as Jamila fires up the engine. It is starting to drizzle, so she secures the roof and decides to head back to GCHQ. Pounding the steering wheel in time to the music, she sings along to the lyrics of *Gettin' Over You*, and pulls out into the early evening traffic.

A Regular Portion of Broccoli*

Mo Wright

Cast your mind back to 1966... was it Thunderball?
Where were you when the magic hit
I was in Sheffield, heavily pregnant
  at a mid-night matinee, great excitement.
The dark swarthy Scot,
With the silver tongue.
The chase
The plot
The suspense
The charm
The near-death tease.
Now fifty years on
  and still they come,
Casino Royale
Quantum of Solace
Skyfall
Spectre

What next?

Sean's reflexes, like mine, are now far from fast
Pierce persona a little faded
Roger the dodger, looks pale and worn.
But Daniel, my hero, will live for ever!
That cut glass jaw,
Those lagoon blue eyes.
His derring-do
The ultimate action man.
Fit and fearless.

**For those not that familiar with James Bond films Mr Albert R. Broccoli was the main producer for many years until he died in 1996.*

Bond to the Rescue

Mo Wright

Are you bonded to Bond?
Do his adventures excite?
Are you one more film buff?
Does he thrill and delight?
There's the derring, the do
The evil intent,
The darker view,

All spy plot – portent!

Do you crave the abyss?
The corrupt the unknown?
Do you thrill at the chase?
Are you murder lust prone?
If the answer is yes,
Then there's nothing to lose.
The Aston Martin has gas.

We are ready to cruise!

Be it Connery or Bronson,
Dodger Moore or our Craig.
You are caught in a cycle,
That's bound to deprave.
So release your constraints,
The nightmares the fears,
Without Bond to protect you,

It may all end in tears!

Home from the Jungle

Frederic Stansfield

James took his tomes on seventeenth century Jamaican piracy back to the desk.

'I'm going there next week to do some field research, so the books can go back to the depository,' he said.

The assistant was Helen, his favourite librarian. She had volunteered part-time in the local library whilst she studied for her degree. In those days she wore flowery white blouses and tight blue jeans. Now that she had a permanent job at the British Library she still wore blue and white; but the blue was a business suit.

'I am going on holiday as well next week,' she said. 'Two days in France.' Then she had to move onto the next reader.

As James went outside for a coffee he heard a familiar voice. It was Silverpound.

'Your perm is more immaculate than ever', James said.

'Thank you, James. D let me have a long lunch hour; but now he wants to see you in the office at once.'

Miss Silverpound led the way to the staff entrance: they were civil servants after all. The Service had sent a car. Less than fifteen minutes later, James was in front of D's desk.

'Glad you could come, Booker.' D said. 'We want you to find out about a Farook Al-Tuffi. He's ruling the roost at The Jungle. We think he is planning a terrorist attack. '

'I'll take the Aston Martin. I can be in Calais in four hours,' James said.

'No, Booker. I'd like you to be discreet, just for once.'

D pressed his buzzer. James went outside to the anteroom desk from which Silverwood organised everything.

'Here are your coach ticket to Dover and ferry ticket to Calais.'

James took a taxi to Victoria Coach Station. There was a queue for Service 007 to Dover. James boarded and took a seat on the offside. A couple of women wearing burkas sat a couple of rows behind him. Then a gaggle of hippies, wearing seventies-style clothes walked past to the back seats. To his astonishment, Helen, back in her blue jeans, was amongst them. She was sandwiched between two men wearing baggy jerseys.

Helen had just time to give James a quick smile. 'I've joined Labour. Momentum have organised a demo,' she said.

As the coach set off across Vauxhall Bridge, past the office and down New Dover Road, the driver played music over the intercom.

'They're playing my tune!' James thought. The hippies all sang along to a medley of songs from the films. James got out his *Times.* He concentrated on solving the last three crossword clues.

When the coach reached the M2, the hippies stopped singing, starting instead to plot about The Jungle. They schemed about how the immigrants could get onto the ferry.

The passengers got off the coach at Dover Ferry Terminal. Once they had boarded the ship, James made for the Club Lounge. He had it to himself. The hippies were all in the bar on the deck below, and the two women in burkas had retreated to an alcove.

'Would you like a drink, sir?' The waiter asked.

'Dry martini. Shaken, not stirred.'

Half way across the Channel, S, wearing his lab coat, poked his nose into the lounge.

'I can't keep you away,' James said.

'I've got a new gadget for you.' It was a mobile phone. James inspected it carefully.

'If you press the camera button twice, it fires a laser.'

James tried it out. A hole appeared in a table on the other side of the lounge.

At Calais, there was a tedious one hundred yard bus journey from ship to terminal. Once there, James was surprised by a familiar Southern drawl.

'Hi, James.' It was Fernando Lietz. 'Let me give you a lift to the hotel.' He led the way to a Chevrolet and they set off.

'I hear you are after Al-Tuffi. The Company are watching him too. He is dangerous. He is smuggling heroin into the States. So let us know if you find out anything.'

James checked in the mirror. The women in burkas were behind, in a chauffeur driven Mercedes with darkened windows.

'We're being followed,' he said.

Lietz accelerated and sped the long way round the town to the hotel. They seemed to have shaken off the Arab women.

'See you later.' Lietz said. 'I've booked a table at *Les Vieux Paysans* at seven.'

The Hotel Hector was a comfortable old building; but it looked as though it had seen better days. The foyer and the corridors were empty.

James carried his own luggage up the curving staircase. He turned the door handle slowly, keeping to the wall as he entered the room.

A girl was lying on the double bed. It was Helen. She was reading a copy of Proust's *In Remembrance of Things Past:* the second volume, *In the Shadow of Young Girls in Flower.* The book was on the pillow. Helen was on her stomach to read it, wearing her blue jeans.

'Hello,' she said. 'I couldn't face being at the hostel with those ghastly protesters.'

James lent over and kissed Helen on the nape of her neck.

'It's time to go for dinner,' James said, an hour later.

Les Vieux Paysans was only round the corner. Fernando Leitz had already taken a table near the window. The only other diners were the two women wearing burkas.

'I'll have a sirloin steak. Medium rare.' Leitz told the waiter. Helen ordered Coq au Vin, and James followed suit. He bought a bottle of the best Bordeaux to go with their meal.

'What makes you want to protest at the Jungle?' James asked Helen.

'Their conditions are terrible. It's our duty to get them to England.'

'It's not so simple, Helen. The traffickers are not very nice people at all.' James didn't have a chance to explain further. Three of the largest hippies from the bus burst through the restaurant doorway.

'Come with us, Helen,' one of them ordered. 'We're going to the English pub.'

Helen looked wistful.

'I've got to be sociable, darling,' she said to James. 'I'll see you tomorrow. Ten o'clock at the Place d'Armes.' She made to hug James, but one of the hippies tore her away.

The two women in burkas followed the hippies out of the restaurant. One of them was talking on her mobile.

The next morning, James dressed in a sweater and informal trousers. He rummaged in his suitcase and found a couple of CND badges to supplement his outfit. Then he went to the Place d'Armes, where about a hundred people had gathered. Helen was there, wearing a head scarf. James made to go over; but one of the large hippies stopped him.

'Your place is at the front.' He gave James a placard saying *Save The Syrians*. 'The girl will walk at the back with the other women. She is none of your business.'

The march set off on the road past the docks. There was nobody around to read their banners and posters. Half an hour later they reached a large barbed wire compound. A phalanx of sullen gendarmes reluctantly let the demonstrators through.

Inside, the camp could have been in a war-torn African country. A line of women were queuing inside the gate to get water from a tap. They would take their pails back to one of hundreds of makeshift, litter-strewn shelters. Listless youths were smoking home-rolled cigarettes, wafting sweet smells of hashish.

The marchers ignored the tents, marching on until they reached a more privileged area with containers. It was dominated by a house fashioned from eight of the metal boxes, four on each of two levels. Outside there was a big white container lorry parked on tarmac beside a neat square lawn.

An enormous, thick-set man marched towards the hippy who was guarding James. He was bare to the waist, wearing a ceremonial straw skirt. But there was nothing ceremonial about his pistol or his three-foot long scimitar.

'Is this one of Al-Tuffi's bodyguards?' James asked. He barely had time to see the man's fist.

When James came to, the blow to his head had left him with a splitting headache; but he slowly realised that he was tied to a hard chair in an otherwise luxuriously furnished and carpeted room. Half a dozen almost identical bodyguards, each stripped to the waist and displaying oiled ebony skin, lined the walls. Between them, Al-Tuffi, wearing a flowing cotton robe, sat behind a large teak desk. An elderly woman stood by his side, wearing a headscarf and holding a long sharp knife. At the far end of the room Helen was strapped to a large diagonal cross.

'Helen is going to work in my kitchens,' Al-Tuffi said. 'But first her face is going to be scarred so that no man will look at her. You might as well watch, Booker. It will be the last thing you'll ever see.'

The elderly woman walked towards Helen with her knife whilst one of the bodyguards, with a ghastly deep laugh, made ready to deal with James.

James had already felt his pocket. The bodyguards had overlooked his mobile. Now, with the supernatural strength of desperation, he pulled his hands free of his bonds. He fired the laser hurriedly. Thank goodness, the shots were accurate. The ropes fell from Helen's wrists. James swivelled and fired at the two bodyguards next to Al-Tuffi, blinding them. Out of the corner of his eye, James saw the next bodyguard raising his scimitar. He jumped at the man's throat to drop him, catching the scimitar as it fell from his hand. He caught the next bodyguard with a kick and then cut his companion in two with the scimitar.

Helen had not been idle. She had knocked the knife from the woman's hand before leaping at the remaining bodyguard, breaking his neck with a kick.

'My self-defence class has come in useful after all,' she said.

'There is no time to lose,' James said, grabbing Helen by the hand. They ran down an external metal staircase and jumped into the cab of the container lorry. James accelerated it through the camp wire as three Mercs gave chase, firing machine guns. Bullets splattered the container. A couple of them slammed into the cab, fortunately missing James and Helen.

A French fast patrol boat was at the quay, raring to sail. Lietz was already there.

'Jump in, James.'

Helen jumped aboard, immediately followed by Helen. They made to sea at high speed; but Al-Tuffi gave chase, firing missiles and machine guns from his helicopter. Helen grabbed a missile launcher and fired. The helicopter crashed onto the patrol boat in a suicide dive. It burst into flames.

Lietz was trying in vain to help the French crew extinguish the fire; but there was no time to wait. James pulled a cord to release an orange inflatable into the sea.

'Here, Helen!' He cried.

Helen grabbed the outboard motor at the stern of the inflatable. In the distance, Dover docks were in sight. She steered towards the harbour entrance.

As the emergency passed, James put his arm around Helen. 'You are going the wrong way,' he said. 'My house is at St. Margaret's Bay.'

When they tied up at the small jetty, Silverpound was waiting.

'I've got some tea for you,' she said. 'A large pot with two cups. And cream scones. You've plenty of time. I've never told D the house is in French mobile space.'

'Let's check out the bedroom first,' Helen said. 'I've had enough of being a librarian.'

James picked up his girl and carried her upstairs. Silverpound sighed.

Beachy Head

Carole Lynch

The two brothers lay as they often did, on their backs on the clifftop, looking up at a cloudless sky. The view from between their feet was of the open sea; the distant horizon unclear as the blue above was reflected in the ocean beneath. Steve, nearest the edge, who was idly chewing grass, rolled over to look at one of the Lloyd-Hartford sisters as she cycled past.

'You've got no chance, mate,' said Ian glancing round. 'Totally out of your league.'

'Oh, I dunno. She's always flashing a bit of leg.'

'What, you reckon she'd fancy a roll in the hay with one of us peasants? In your dreams, sunshine.'

'As soon as I can I'm getting out of this dump. I'm not always going to be just one of the local yokels.'

Ian rolled onto his stomach and punched his brother on the arm. 'Who are you calling a yokel?' He frowned. 'Anyway, what's wrong with it? You always think the grass is greener somewhere else. It really isn't.'

Steve snorted. 'You'd know would you? God, you sound just like Dad. If I get the grades, I'm off to university next year. Freedom. No more "put that damn radio off we're trying to get to sleep in here."' He spat out the grass, shrugged himself into a sitting position and looked over at the lighthouse. Ian followed his gaze.

'You're lucky. Can't see me doing much in the exams. I was thinking of an apprenticeship. Dad says he'll take me on at the garage if I want.'

Steve rolled his eyes in an eloquent gesture. He'd long considered his brother a lost cause. 'Let's go on the front and play the slots,' was all he said in response.

The trading floor was buzzing; screens were changing moment by moment, prices falling. Steven was thirsty, but daren't leave his desk in case he missed his moment. The back of his neck was tingling. Was this it? It was like watching for the wave at Thurso East. Taking a deep breath, he grabbed the phone, dialled and spoke rapidly, agreeing quantity and price per barrel. There was an agonising wait. Steven paced, drummed his fingers on the desk, sipped water. Then up it flashed – an announcement from OPEC that they would no longer increase production. He stared at the figures as they immediately began to climb. His armpits were damp. Now he was riding the wave. His hand hovered over the phone; waited for the end of the upswing. Another negotiation. He'd done it. Another large bonus in the bag. He was wired; on a roll; still the company golden boy. Steven slumped back in his chair, trembling.

After work, a group of them piled into their favourite bar. Noise levels were high as Cristal Champagne flowed and deals were offered up for congratulation. Steven felt a great sense of belonging as he footed the bill, yet again, like a golfer must feel after a hole in one.

He was smiling as he said goodnight to the doorman on the way up to his penthouse apartment. Steven noticed as she greeted him that Cassie was again wearing something new. There were bags from designer stores beside the sofa.

'You've had a good day, I can tell,' she said, eyes sparkling like the jewel around her neck. She moved against his body as she reached up for him.

'Ah,' he murmured. 'My reward.'

His mobile vibrated. Steven glanced at the screen. It was Ian. He felt under pressure, didn't have time to listen to stories of how great being a father was or how good his marriage to Mandy. He pressed 'can't talk now.' They hadn't spoken for a long time. Steven knew the fault was his. He'd lost count of the number of occasions he'd blocked the call in response to his brother's attempts to stay in touch. Didn't Ian realise that he'd moved on, that they no longer had anything in common? He received a text. 'Dad ill. Stroke. Probably best if you come soon.' Without giving it much thought, Steven texted back, 'Not good time to be away from work at the mo. Will try.'

A cheer went up behind him. Steven didn't bother to look round. It would be the new golden boy making a killing. He felt sick. It had been a while since he'd picked up the bar tab. A wave of fatigue hit him. His body felt heavy with the realisation that he was losing it.

After a fruitless day spent on the phone, Steven walked slowly into the lift. In his hand was the post, most of which he recognised as bills. As the doors opened into the sitting room, Cassie came over to him brandishing a statement.

'What the hell, Steven? My card was refused in Armani. I've never been so embarrassed in my life. Pay off the balance, now, will you?'

'Well. Nice to see you, too.'

She glared at him. He just stood and looked back at her.

'You look odd. What's happened? What's going on?'

He threw the envelopes at her. 'Here, put that demand for money with all the others. Form a queue behind the mortgage arrears, the car loans and all the other bits of plastic you flash around on a whim for things you don't bloody need, things you only buy because your friends have got one.'

Cassie stood with her mouth open, for once speechless. Steven turned and headed for the shower. He'd only got as far as the bedroom before Cassie, panicked, started to fling questions at him. He put up a hand.

'Oh, stop it, for God's sake. Get us some drinks - large ones. You're going to need it and I plan on getting drunk.'

Steven explained that he'd lost his job a while ago and since then had been sitting in coffee houses phoning all his contacts and other leads, trying to get another one. Cassie took a gulp of whisky.

'So what's the problem?'

'It's the reason I was fired. Nobody will touch me with a bargepole; crap reference.'

Cassie looked confused. 'Just tell me.'

So he explained that he'd lost his touch; how living on adrenaline for so long caused him to burn out; how he'd been driven to steal to get an edge; the constant pressure to maintain their lifestyle.

'Steal? Steal what?'

'Only the ten-year strategic plan of a competitor. Nothing really.' His hollow laugh only increased her anxiety.

'How did you get it? Why weren't the company pleased?'

This was the question he'd hoped not to be asked. He wouldn't meet her eyes. 'You don't want to know, really you don't.' He felt a moment's gratitude that legal proceedings against him had not been instigated.

'So there was another woman, then?'

Ian passed the potatoes to his brother. 'Come on mate, you've got to eat.'

Steven took just one as he continued to tell the story. 'So that was it. No understanding. No support. She was off.'

Mandy put her hand on his. 'I'm so sorry, Steve. She obviously didn't really love you then.'

He spat out a laugh so brittle it seemed as if it might splinter into a thousand pieces. 'Real? I don't know that any of it was real.' They ate in silence for a while. 'Look,' he said. 'I'm sorry to dump myself on you. I've lost everything and I've nowhere else to go.'

'We're family. Of course you came to us.' Ian smiled to push home the message.

The next morning, Steven woke to an audience of two small people sitting on his bed.

'Get up, sleepy head. Will you take us to the funfair, Uncle Steve, pleeease?'

He groaned and opened his eyes. 'What time is it?'

'Mummy says it's time for you to be up.' This from Alice, who at eight had often shown that she was a born organiser. She pulled at the quilt. Steven gripped it modestly and shooed them out while he got dressed. He had no idea what to do, having had no experience with children. Alice seemed to sense this, and told her brother to hold his uncle's hand while she chatted about their lives as they walked along. She asked questions too. 'Did you live here with Daddy when you were a boy,' followed up with 'why did you go away, then?'

Steven struggled to answer, was beginning to wonder himself. As the afternoon wore on he relaxed and found that he was enjoying the children's company. He had nothing to prove; they simply accepted him. They were all laughing as they fell into the kitchen back at the house. Before bed, both children hugged their Uncle Steve and thanked him for a great time. He couldn't get any words out; just held on to them both tightly for far too long. He got up abruptly and told Mandy he was going out for a walk.

The wind was getting up as Steven made his way to the High Street. He recognised some of the shops and pubs, but dotted here and there others were new. He hadn't been aware of the changes. As he made his way down towards the headland, he heard someone calling him.

'Good Lord. If it isn't Steve. How are you, mate? It must be years.'

He turned to see Dave, one of his friends from school, grinning at him. 'Hey,' he said. 'How are things with you? It's been ages.'

They chatted for a few minutes. He discovered that Dave had qualified as a Pharmacist and owned a chain of Chemist shops.

'No,' Steve said in answer to the inevitable question. 'No kids - too busy. All much too late now.' Pain gnawed at his guts.

'Give me your number,' Dave said. 'Let's get together for a drink. God, it's so good to see you.'

Steve walked on and checked his mobile. There were still no texts or emails; none of his friends in London had responded to his messages. So he was a pariah, then. He watched as a stray dog loped aimlessly along the street, tail down, looking for scraps, barely surviving.

He found himself approaching the cliffs. The light was fading and the wind had whipped up a gale. Steve leaned into it, trying to stay on his feet. Just planting one foot in front of the other was all he could do. The storm screamed around his ears, he could hardly breathe for the force of it. Progress was slow, but he made it to the top. He watched, mesmerised, as the water below churned, crashing against the blackness of the rocks, a rip tide sucking at everything in its path, dragging it down. A hand grabbed his arm and gripped it firmly.

'I knew I'd find you here.' Ian shouted above the din. 'You always were too close to the edge.'

Steve turned and tried to free himself to no avail. He gave up. 'I never got to see the old man before he died,' he howled. 'Far too busy with much more important things. I'm so sorry.'

'He knew he'd lost you when you got your exam results,' Ian bellowed. 'He was so proud of you. I was jealous.'

Steve, amazed, turned to look at his brother. 'But I was always envious of you because I thought you were his favourite – he did give you a job. He never lifted a finger to help me. Ever.'

The wind began to abate and Ian didn't have to shout as loud for Steve to hear him. 'You were clever, mate, didn't need his help. But me? I'd have been sunk without it.'

Steven put his hand in his pocket and pulled out his business card. Keeping hold of it, nail beds white with the strength of his grip, he showed it to Ian, who squinting at it in the fading light, read, 'Steven M Diamond, Commodities Trader.' There was a moment, then he opened his fingers and let go. Steve watched as the breeze randomly tossed the embossed cardboard in the air. Then it was gone. The lighthouse flashed.

Ian pulled gently on his brother's arm. 'It's time to come home.'

'Why are you doing this when I'm such a shit?'

'We're brothers. And, as we used to say when we were kids, 'Diamonds are forever.''

The cliff at Beachy Head is 531 feet high; there is a telephone box there showing the Samaritans number.

The Man with the Golden Heart

Carol Hyde

Every day at skyfall, I peak through the lace curtains to see if my Bertie is on his way home. He's a bus driver, so he appreciates the long walk home from the depot, after sitting on his bum all day. If I spot him coming along the way, I can't help smiling. He's the love of my life, is Bertie.

I was on my own for several years before he came along, and I've been counting my lucky stars ever since. My first husband took off with someone half his age, and I thought I'd never get over it. I was very depressed for a long time, and the doctor wanted to give me antidepressants, but I don't like taking pills so I put my foot down and said, 'Dr, No!'

But I was so lonely, and when Bertie came along he was my quantum of solace. He lifted me out of despair and put me up on a pedestal. I remember when he asked me to marry him – to make a decent woman of me, he said, joking of course. Well, I nearly fainted. All through dinner - his favourite, steak and kidney pie - he had a real twinkle in his eye, so after dinner I said 'What's up, Golden Eye?'

I could see he was bursting to say something, but instead, he got down on his knee in front of me, sitting on the sofa, and opened up a little box. I screamed with surprise. I'd never seen such a beautiful ring.

'Diamonds are forever, you know that, don't you darlin'?' he said.

'Oh Bertie,' I said, 'you must have a gold finger to be able to afford something so huge!'

'The world is not enough for a lady like you,' he said, 'but I hope you'll accept this and agree to be my wife.' He was ever so solemn.

Well, it suddenly hit me like a thunderball. This lovely man wanted to marry me and spend the rest of his life with me. I was so excited I didn't know whether to laugh or cry, so I did both. But when he saw my tears, he thought I was going to say no.

'Yes, yes, yes!' I yelled, jumping up and down around the lounge room, and his eyes opened wide with relief.

'You scared the living daylights out of me for a moment, with your crying. I thought you were going to say no.'

I sobered for a moment, and said, 'Oh love, you know how much I love you and how happy this makes me, but you know I've been let down before. Will you promise me I'm not going to wake up one day and find you've gone?'

'Cath,' he said, looking at me very sternly, 'what's done is done, you have to let go of the past. It's up to you to live and let die. So yes, for your eyes only, forever, cross my heart.' He smiled at me and wiped away my tears and then I threw myself at him so hard, we both fell backwards onto the sofa and we roared with laughter.

Well, I won't go into what happened after that, but things got very cosy indeed. In the morning, we stayed in bed late, 'cause it was his day off. He asked me where I'd like to go for the honeymoon. I think I said something like Brighton, but then he surprised me with two tickets to Monte Carlo, where we would be staying at the Casino Royale, no less. I don't think we got out of bed until two in the afternoon after that lovely surprise. We were really hot for each other back then. He used to call me his little octopussy, and said he wanted us to make love eight days a week.

That was ten years ago, and while the sex may not be what it used to be, I've never regretted marrying him for a single moment. He's been so good to me, and so helpful around the house too, not like other men his age. He loves our little garden and keeping everything looking nice.

One evening I was lying in the bath, when I thought I heard the mower going outside. I told myself I must be imagining it, because it was already quite dark out. Eventually the noise stopped and I called out to Bertie, to see what he was up to. When he didn't answer, I climbed out of the bath, wrapped a towel around me and went to see where he was. Sure enough, there he was, out in the dark, raking up the grass.

'What are you doing, ya daft fella?' I called.

'Well, if we're going away in the morning, I have to get the garden cleaned up, or it will be too overgrown by the time we get back.'

'So you're a bus driver by day and a moonraker by night, is that it? Come inside love, you've done enough for one day.' He still loves to keep busy and has no intention of slowing down.

He's a bit of a philosopher too, sometimes. He said to me one day, 'I hope this idea of being born again is right, because I'd love to live another life with you.'

'You? Only live twice? I think someone as lovely as you should live forever. The world could do with more men like you.' Oh he does make me laugh.

Another time he said, 'I'm going to love you tomorrow and tomorrow and tomorrow. You know why?'

'Why?' I asked.

'Because tomorrow never dies.' He is such a romantic sometimes.

I don't know what I'd do if anything happened to him. He did give me a fright a couple of years back. He had a bit of a turn when he was at work. Thankfully he hadn't yet taken the bus out. The doctor said he had a mild heart attack, which shocked us both. He was only fifty-two.

When I brought him home from the hospital, we were sitting in the back of the taxi, when he put his hand over mine, and said quietly, 'Don't you worry love, I'm not going to leave any time soon. I'll die another day, and it will be a long time from now, that's for sure.'

The spectre of him gone hung in the air in front of me, and I clung to him tightly. 'Please God, let this man go on forever.'

Beige

Emma Collins

If she had to compare herself to a colour it would have to be beige. A bland, neutral, nothing kind of colour. She'd realised this years ago and it wasn't a fact that upset her anymore. She laughed, joked, cried and participated as much as the rest but hand on heart she didn't have strong opinions about anything... except bread. Refrigerated bread, actually.

Her main focus of this hatred were petrol garages. The job took her up and down cement highways that snaked around the UK. No matter how hard she planned ahead she always seemed to be caught out near the depressing seventies service stations that were crying out for a bit of regeneration. The new swish ones were always a bit too far, no matter how much she marvelled at the idea of an actual Nandos or Burger King in these depressing spots. No, invariably she ended up at one of the shittier garages clutching a forlorn sandwich she'd grabbed from the back hoping it was slightly fresher than the one in front. Nearly four pounds now for bread with only the cut lined with filling to make it look plentiful. Then the first bite and the remembered horror of why she hated cold, dank bread.

Today was a good day; she had the foresight to swing past McDonalds and feasted on a McMuffin and strong coffee before hitting the road. No cold bread today.

She was on her way to Luton. Ready to mill around the streets, try and get as close to the leaders as possible but if that failed she would settle for listening and chatting to the protesters, sometimes the best bits of intelligence were from the foot soldiers. She looked suitably reporter-ish. Her average brown hair tied back in a neat ponytail, a lick of makeup, low heeled brown boots, a thin jacket (in beige of course). Her press association badge was in her case ready to be slipped on. She had her camera (hidden and official) charged up and her Moleskine notebook which was a must for any pretend journo.

She was glad she was on assignment and out of the office. It may have been only three floors up from where she'd started off as a data analysist but it could have been a different world. Dominated by men in flash suits and silly watches, she didn't belong. They knew it and she knew it. Where they were all midnight informant meets, shadowy clubs and high-tech gadgets, she just did what she did best and blended. Which method was best was yet to be seen.

She passed the first Luton exit, chose the next instead, and went directly to the Bury Park area. The march wasn't due to pass for hours but the police presence was already heavy. They waved her towards the marked diversion and while she sat and waited her turn to go through she took a quick look at her notes. Same old players, warming up in the wings right now she thought, desperate to take centre stage.

EDL, Muslim4UK, Militant anti-fascists and perhaps a peppering of good old fashioned Nazis to really get things bubbling. She wished they could see how disgustingly similar they all were to each other, laughable that they thought they were all so different. She thought of the 'fatwa' issued by an EDL man to a journalist who had exposed links to Combat 18. She supposed no one knew who they were really hating anymore or why. The Fatwa had made her chuckle though, nothing like confusingly borrowing a bit of your enemy's ideology.

She had her eye on two or three of the EDL men today. Intel had suggested that they were strengthening links to a military group in America. Kingdom Identity, as they were currently calling themselves, were reaching out, calling for their white supremacy brothers to organise.

The diversion had lead them out of the high street area and past a bingo hall, that was once called Mecca. A letter box bomb a few years ago had put an end to that particular incarnation and now the sign simply read Bingo Hall. She knew the area pretty well by now and was sure she would end up miles away from where she wanted to be so she began to break away from the traffic, twisting her little car around the back streets until she was behind a boarded up old shop. She parked and ignoring the No Parking sign began to walk back to where, at midday, the English Defence League planned to march.

At the first police cordon she passed by unnoticed and it wasn't until she got to the march route that a policewoman asked her for ID. She flashed her press card and walked towards the town hall. Two men wearing suits were setting up a temporary stage for their leader to speak from. One of the men kept pulling at his collar obviously uncomfortable and not very at home in his suit. Jimmy Fadden was trying to present his party as a legitimate choice. He was desperate to get away from the image of the stereotypical Doctor Martin booted tattooed skinheads. If you wanted to be in Jimmy Fadden's inner circle a nice suit was a good start.

'So, where's the big man?' she called over to the two goons.

The smaller one began to walk over to her and she recognised him as Scott Michaels. A light scar that drifted from his lip to the corner of his left eye almost gave the impression he was smiling. She knew though this was certainly not a kindly older man. His file was thick and not a pleasant read.

'What's it to you? He'll be here when he needs to be here.' He was next to her now.

'Jenna Simpson.' She offered her hand and he shook it limply. 'I work for IPS.' He looked blank and she continued, 'It's the biggest independent news service in the world. We tell the news as it really is, not how people think it should be told.' She was in character now. Jenna was ballsy, intelligent and sexy so for now that's would she would be. Scott looked at her hard as if seeing her for the first time.

'Oh yeah?' A lascivious smile spread across his face and he looked her up and down slowly. 'Yeah, I know IPS. James has it on his list of agencies he wants to speak to about our cause. Hang on, let me call him and see if he wants to chat.'

She forced herself to flash a big smile at him. 'No prob, sweetie.'

He walked off tapping on his mobile. Scott Michaels was a pig but he was nothing compared to Jimmy or James as he was calling himself. He had nearly succeeded in legitimising the severe Right Wing with lots of people. That he was young, good looking and articulate had aroused interest abroad. Any extremist group is trouble but with international chapters springing up, the agency had decided to move quick. It was information gathering time so the correct people could be stamped out.

Jenna, as she was now, began to write in her note book and took some photos for effect. Scott was nodding and talking, still out of hearing distance but he kept glancing over at her. He finally began to walk back towards her and ended the call. 'Jim - James has some time. He asked you to meet him at the hotel he's getting ready in, said you could have breakfast together.'

'Great. Great stuff,' she trilled sweetly. 'Where's the hotel?'

'I'll take you.'

'It's not necessary, I have Google maps.' She managed a little chuckle.

'Nah. I'm not letting a lovely young lady like you walk about here on your own, not with all these types floating about.' He gestured to a tired-looking shop keeper who had begun to board up his shop.

She shuddered inwardly but said brightly for them to go. It was nearly nine and she was desperate to try and get some time with Jimmy and eyeball who his close associates were at the moment.

She tried to chat during the ten-minute walk to the Thistle hotel on the other side of the town centre, but Scott barely replied. He brushed against her thigh as often as possible though and she felt edgy. When they reached the hotel she was relieved but he lead the way to a lift.

'Floor ten,' he barked, and she dutifully pressed the button. The lift started with a lurch and he pretended to fall against her.

She firmly pushed him back. 'Don't do this, you're meant to be charming me,' she warned.

Anger contorted his face. 'You stuck up little bitch.' The lift opened and Scott pushed her out. The strap of her bag caught in her boot and she fell out of the lift into a heap on the floor. The wind knocked out of her lungs.

'What the hell's going on here?' A man came flying out of one of the doors, pushing Scott by the throat back into the lift.

'I'm sorry! She just tripped on her bag.'

'I've warned you, Scotty. Play the game nicely or you can fuck off!' He came back to where she was trying to get up from the floor. He put out his hand and pulled her gently to her feet. He towered over her.

'Jenna' she said wincing, holding out her hand.

'Jimmy' he said shaking her hand. 'Pleasure to meet you.' He was big, handsome and incredibly male and when he looked at her it was like he could really see her. And suddenly she didn't feel beige any more.

I Should've Gone To Marks...

Judy Walker

Honor was after a sweater; pure wool, polo neck, easy wash. She didn't care what colour so long as it was cheap. She just wanted to stay warm when she walked the dogs these chilly mornings. She should have gone to Marks...

Instead, she went to TJ MAX and started riffling through the racks. There were lots of sweaters – funny sizes, lurid colours, rough acrylic, bizarre designs – rows of them. Then she spotted it. It hung alone on a display peg so high she had to stretch and reach on tip-toe to pull it down. It wasn't too expensive. She checked the size and what it was made of, scrutinized the washing instructions. It was black. It would go with anything. It looked perfect – just what she wanted. It was almost too good to be true. It was so good - she'd better try it on just to make sure.

She had to wait in a queue to get into the changing room. It was hot – very hot, especially wearing her bulky coat. There were half a dozen women in front of her making a run on a new consignment of evening wear – Christmas parties – lucky devils! *Not too much glamour in my life*, thought Honor. The queuing women clutched long evening dresses in bright colours. The pretty girl directly in front was minutely examining the sequined bodice of the turquoise, off-the-shoulder number she'd chosen. It was exactly the right colouring for her.

It took forever to get a number tag and locate an empty cubicle. She was glad to slip off her coat and boots; she was sweltering. She was struggling to get the pullover she was wearing over her head when she suddenly felt fuzzy. It was a sudden flush of heat and dizziness that made her reel. She shot out a hand to steady herself and dissolved through the mirror. It was the weirdest feeling.

She was in a dim corridor with a red swirling carpet on the floor. The rough fibers scratched against her cheek. She sat up feeling exposed and silly to be wearing just her bra and jeans. It wasn't even her new push-up bra. She looked up and saw a line of photos. They were all of good looking, suave men wearing dinner jackets. Each seemed to be draped in slender, beautiful girls wearing pouts but little else. The photos stretched all the way along to a door at the far end.

A long turquoise evening gown with sequined bodice appeared with the girl-in-front wearing it. She had a mask of pale make-up and jewelry that sparkling even in this dim light.

'Oh dear,' said the girl, 'you can't carry on like that. That's atrocious. Here, let me help you.'

Honor struggled to wrap the gauzy stole around herself, hiding her tatty bra as much as possible and followed turquoise and sequins to the door at the end of the corridor. Stepping through she was near blinded by light. It was all-round glitter and glitz. Prisms of light reflected off massive ceiling chandeliers and danced around the red and gold flock walls. Sumptuous. That was the word that came to her mind. The next word Honor thought of was *noise*. She heard the combined volume of female voices shrieking, laughing and chattering, a clink - like hard ice falling into glasses, the sudden pop - of a cork, the rattle, likely a ball spinning round a roulette wheel, a croupier saying: 'It's all red.' The air was brimming with perfume and after-shave lotion lying heavy in the atmosphere like a thick morning fog over the motorway. Honor breathed it in and felt fuzzy again.

Across the room she noticed a handsome, well-shouldered man wearing a white dinner jacket and immaculately pressed trousers speaking tersely to turquoise and sequins. *I know that face* she thought but she couldn't place it; Sean, Daniel, Roger? Who the hell was he? Turquoise and sequins half turned away from him and seemed to be talking into her elegant phone held in her pretty manicured hand. A thick-set, neckless, shiny-pated man dressed in dark navy seated at the baize table turned his head to observe her. He watched for half a minute then stood up, rounding to stare directly at Honor. His eyes bored straight through to her saggy bra. He took a step towards her.

Embarrassed, Honor turned and ran back to the corridor door. Behind her there was a loud crash, a sudden acrid smell, people shouting but she didn't stop.

'Are you alright love?' said a voice. 'Can you hear me? Stay still, the Manager's called an ambulance.'

Too late - Honor was hovering a long way above the fractured shards of mirror and the blood red carpet. 'I should've gone to Marks and Sparks,' she thought.

Live and Let Die

C A Nitzsche

'Do you believe in reincarnation, Madam?'

'What...? Sorry, say that again - I couldn't catch it!' I strained to hear, against the whistling of the wind in my ears, but it was useless. The Land Rover skidded to avoid a goat crossing the road and I lurched forward, clutching at the dashboard, to save myself from hurtling through the windscreen. I turned to face the young Doctor, sitting behind me.

He repeated the question. His eyes were fixed intently on my face. It was an unexpected query. I had considered the topic of reincarnation in the past, but briefly, and in a very cursory manner. In all honesty, I could only reply:

'Sometimes, I do.'

My friend, Ellie, our statistician, tittered at this. She was sitting in the back seat, fanning herself with the spare handouts from the lecture we had just given. I looked at them both:

'I know that sounds odd, but it's true. Sometimes reincarnation seems the only sensible answer. One continuous cycle of life and death and rebirth – recycling. One life is ended and another created. The dance of Shiva!'

The young Doctor smiled at my mention of the God, Shiva, and jiggled his head from side to side in assent. 'I too, believe in reincarnation.'

I smiled back at him. The conversation petered out. It was almost impossible to discuss anything, let alone such a complex subject, whilst we were journeying along these rough, uneven, dirt roads. All other sounds were blotted out by the din of jolting wheels and air whizzing past as we sped along, with now and then, the squawk of chickens as they escaped sudden death beneath our wheels. Death was all around us in this vibrant, colourful, chaotic land of great beauty. Death, but also, fecundity and new life

I thought back to the newborn baby whose birth I had witnessed earlier in the day, just as I entered a rural hospital. The mother lay on a litter. No doctor or nurse was present. She was attended by a cleaner who delivered the baby safely and then, with the utmost care, placed the naked child on a cold, metal tray. The mother appeared miserable and exhausted, rather than elated. She turned her head to the wall and covered her face with her thin cotton sari. I gave instructions for the baby to be wrapped up and placed in its mother's arms, otherwise the warmth of life would drain away from the tiny form. I hoped the close embrace would forge the nurturing bond between mother and child, but there was no immediate response from the woman. I had grave misgivings regarding the child's future. To me, the baby seemed doomed to die before it had even existed. Here, such tragic bereavement was often accepted, fatalistically, as being part of life.

Death was so commonplace that infants could only achieve personhood if they survived to nine months of age. All things were passing. But, Christian and Hindu attitudes were not so dissimilar: 'The Lord giveth and the Lord taketh; Blessed be the Name of the Lord!'

The Land Rover braked. We had reached our lodgings. Ellie and I climbed down from the vehicle and waved goodbye to the remaining occupants. A rickshaw wallah was waiting for us by the gate to the house. He carried our lunch which he had brought from the Chinese restaurant. I peered inside the tiffin carrier with some trepidation. As I had half expected, it contained chicken wings and feet, partially camouflaged in a vivid sweet and sour sauce, looking like some blooded Voodoo offering. I carried the unappetising meal into the house, where our colleague, Terry, was sitting at the table, still in his string vest. It was very hot and humid, 41^0C and 100% humidity, without air conditioning. It was the kind of stifling, swelteringly high temperature from which there was no escape; Monsoon weather that inevitably brought with it the discomfort of prickly heat. It was like living in a glasshouse.

Terry inspected the contents of the tiffin carrier and grinned at me: 'Maybe chicken feet safer than chicken meat! Chickens bad for tummy troubles.' He patted his stomach, and laughed.

The three of us, who were organising a number of courses on Community Medicine, were sitting in the house that evening, together with our friend, Phil, the Obstetrics Guru. We had nicknamed Phil *Jenningsji*, as he had taken to wearing a Dhoti in this oppressive weather. We were celebrating the end of the course. Inevitably, later that evening, we were joined by a number of our students, mostly local

Paediatric Consultants, who had come for a chat and to enjoy a cup of coffee, or a glass of lime juice and water, before they said goodbye to us. Some brought small containers of food with snacks or sweetmeats in them.

'We'll be back soon,' we told them, 'and next time some of you will be doing the teaching!'

They were delighted to hear this news. It was a compliment to their skills and presentational abilities, and, more importantly perhaps, lecturing would help them in their career development.

Despite our hopes and good intentions, however, we did not make a speedy return as we had promised. Although we were used to the vagaries of Governments and Politicians, we had not foreseen that they would suddenly call a halt to our teaching programme. It was not until our return to England that we learnt about what, at the time, we presumed, was a temporary hiatus. I busied myself with the other teaching projects and was pleased to see several of my old friends on our new course on Maternal and Child Health.

I was chatting to one of the lecturers after the morning's work, as we had lunch together. He was a retired Obstetrician who had spent many years working in India. I told him how our programme had been temporarily suspended and that we did not know why.

'Don't worry,' he said. 'It's just politics. When I was working for the World Health Organisation, at any one time, half of us would be kicking our heels outside the country, somewhere close, in a neighbouring country, waiting for the Government to give us a visa. They like to flex their muscles!'

The Government seemed to spend a long time flexing its muscles and I was kicking my heels in England for quite a while. One of my former students, the star pupil, wrote to tell me that he had been offered a very well paid job in the Gulf. He was in a quandary. He did not know whether to accept the post or not. It would obviously be better for his family if he took up the job offer, but he felt he owed it to us to participate in the teaching programme. He wanted to make his contribution to it.

I was anxious to resume teaching, both for my own sake and that of the students. We had all put a great deal of effort into our training and this work was now about to bear fruit. I went to see the Dean and asked him if the diplomatic overtures had been successful and whether any progress had been made.

'None at all,' he replied. 'Personally, I think the teaching programme is finished. No chance whatsoever of it continuing.'

When I suggested that I could go out and see if anything could be done to resuscitate the programme, he was adamant that I was not to go. I saw that there was no point in pleading with him. I had no choice but to bide my time. I wrote to the star pupil saying that the prospects for the course continuing were not good, but that I would try to come out, if permitted. Although I was sad to lose him, I advised him to take up the job in the Gulf for the sake of his family. After a couple of weeks, a second student wrote to say that he, too, had been offered a job in the Gulf. There was no time to lose. I visited the Dean once more, this time to ask if I could pack up our personal effects, which were still in the rented house. I offered to make the necessary arrangements for leaving, and to begin writing a report for the

Ministry of Health. He agreed. Two days later, I was on my way to India again.

I arrived at the house in the evening of the following day. I had informed my landlady in advance of my arrival. Almost as soon as I stepped though the door she came down to see me, and shortly afterwards several of the students also flocked in to welcome me back.

They asked me why I had been away for so long and when the next course would start. I explained that it appeared that the Government did not want the teaching programme to continue and that I had returned only in order to pack up our belongings. My disappointment was obvious, an emotion that they also shared.

'Haven't you tried to persuade them to let the programme continue?' They asked.

'The Dean and the Overseas Development people have been in contact with the Ministry here...' I began, but they interrupted me:

'No, No,' they chorused, 'You need to go to the top, things only move at the top in India, nothing ever happens below that level.'

'But the Ministry of Health is the top!' I protested.

'No, No! They are not the top, only the middle! You need to see the Chief Minister for the State. We can arrange it for you as Dr Sharma, here, is related to him, and your landlady, Mrs Singh, knows him well. Dr Sharma and Mrs Singh will speak with him tonight. You can go first thing tomorrow, but do not take your driver and do not let anyone at the Ministry know. Just call a rickshaw wallah off the street and ask him to take you to the Minister's residence, the Raj Bhavan.'

Later that night, I received a message from Mrs Singh to say that the Minister of State was ready to see me at 8am the following day. Accordingly, I took a rickshaw early the next morning to the Raj Bhavan. Guards stood to attention and I was ushered into the presence of the Minister, a tall, imposing man with an impassive countenance. He did not comment or question me as I explained to him why I thought that the teaching programme was important and why it should continue. I gazed demurely at the floor, as I spoke, hoping that this would show my respect for his status. When I had finished speaking, he thought for a moment, then nodded his head, but said nothing. I was dismissed. I thanked him for listening to me and then left, returning with the rickshaw wallah who had been waiting outside. Later that morning, around lunch time, I visited the local hospital to see the Hospital Superintendent, a close associate of the Minister of Health. He was sitting in his office, chatting to the Deputy Superintendant who was a friend of mine. They both beamed at me. They were in very good spirits.

'Good news, Good news!' the Superintendent greeted me. 'We have just heard from Delhi. The approval for the teaching programme to continue has come though, even now, about half an hour ago. You can start as soon as possible!'

I was amazed, delighted and impressed at the speed and efficacy of my friends' intervention. I thanked the Superintendent profusely and through him, I thanked the Minister for his kindness. My Indian friends and I were elated. The teaching and training programmes recommenced almost immediately

I only saw the Minister once again. The Overseas Aid Department had decided that it was best to call a halt to the Project after the next two courses. No further funding would be forthcoming. There was no point in remonstrating- the accountants had decreed that it should finish and their word was final. It was at the farewell ceremony that I saw the Chief Minister again. He came for a fleeting visit to see us. Again, he said nothing, but stared hard at me, while one of the Indian Officials welcomed him. This time, I too said nothing. I gazed downwards, not meeting his eyes, as he was told that we were now leaving and that the teaching programme was finished. This time, I knew that the programme had finally been terminated. It had died the death. Shiva, the Destroyer, had danced, but, alas, there was no Creator, no Chief Minister in England whom I could access through friends, in order to reanimate the corpse. The accountants had spoken; their word was law. They would thrive and survive, and the poor would continue to suffer and die. Live and let die was the way of the world.

Author biographies

Brought up in care, **Caroline Cannons** graduated from Sheffield University in 1979 and worked in education for over thirty years. Her short stories for adults and children are published in numerous anthologies. A founder member of Canterbury Yarners, she promotes creative writing for all through public readings of her work.

Emma Collins is an avid reader and as a result of this passion for words began to write her own short stories from a young age. Her master plan is to give this all up when her blockbuster novel (as yet unwritten) is made into a blockbuster film.

Jo Gamgee's interests are music, languages, singing, reading, writing and walking. Her book *German for Musicians* (Faber) was written while teaching at the Royal Northern College of Music. Where would she be without books? Let's just say that the year in which all her books were in storage was a testing time. As a writer, Jo enjoys the sense of being alone and yet not alone. Readers know all about this.

Carol Hyde hails from Australia where she completed two degrees; the second in creative writing. She has had a number of feature articles published. Her stories in this anthology are the first of her fiction work to be published. Carol's aim is to entertain herself and others through short stories – oh, and world domination.

Carole Lynch published two text books, taught Psychology, and worked in the NHS before writing full time. Her short stories can be found in various publications and, as a founder member of the Canterbury Yarners, she regularly reads her work at literary festivals and other venues. She is currently preparing a short story collection.

Valerie Moffit grew up in Northumberland and still misses the hills and coastline of home. After a career in the civil service she is pleased to be jubilada and to have more time to spend learning Spanish, singing and writing stories. She is also researching the history of her Newcastle family.

Susan Morley always had a fascination with words. She loved writing and reciting poetry by heart as a child. She trained as a Drama teacher. After leaving teaching she completed an M.A. in Creative Writing in 2008 where she began writing a family memoir that she would like to publish.

Corry Nitzsche is a retired Doctor who has lived and worked abroad, mainly in Africa, for many years. She has wanted to write since the age of six, but apart from publishing scientific papers and the odd poem, she has only recently managed to start fulfilling that childhood ambition. She has contributed to several anthologies of the CAE creative writers.

John O'Connor lives in the heart of Kent with his wife, teenage daughter, four goldfish, three African land snails and a Border Collie called Whisper. The numbers for the smaller animals may vary from time to time; the others hopefully won't. A constant, nagging desire to write has led to an eclectic mix of short stories, half-finished books and many scraps of paper.

Frederic Stansfield moved to Ramsgate last year. Previously he lived in Canterbury. His most recent work was as a telephone operative in a call centre. He has also been a systems analyst and a university researcher. Frederic has previously published stories in Canterbury Yarns and poetry for SaveAs.

Judy Walker, retired Civil Servant, grandmother of two beautiful boys, lives quietly in Faversham with her brindle French Bulldogs. She likes to escape into her imagination when she writes but finds she is easily distracted by domestic chores.

Mo Wright has written poetry and short stories for a number of years. She recently had two of her poems and a short story published. She grew up in the Home Counties. Living in Surrey then Sussex. She has one son and retired to Kent in 2003.